American Patterns

Acquiring Cultural Awareness and Reading Skills

Kenji Kitao
Vincent Broderick
Barbara Fujiwara
S. Kathleen Kitao
Hideo Miyamoto
Leslie Sackett

 ADDISON-WESLEY PUBLISHERS JAPAN LTD.
Tokyo • Reading, Massachusetts • Menlo Park, California
Don Mills, Ontario • Wokingham, England • Amsterdam
Sydney • Singapore • Mexico City • Bogota • Santiago
San Juan

A Publication of the World Language Division
Editorial: Claire Vivian Smith
Design: Bonnie Chayes Yousefian

Text acknowledgments: p. 41, reprinted courtesy of The Boston Globe; pp. 55–56, reprinted by permission of Ann Landers and the Field Newspaper Syndicate; pp. 62–63, reprinted courtesy of The Boston Globe; pp. 70–72, from *The Hopis: Portrait of a Desert People* by Walter Collins O'Kane. Copyright 1953 by the University of Oklahoma Press; p. 109, from *The Poetry of Robert Frost* edited by Edward Connery Lathem. Copyright 1923, © 1969 by Holt, Rinehart and Winston. Copyright 1951 by Robert Frost. Reprinted by permission of Holt, Rinehart and Winston, Publishers; pp. 115–116, "Quince Jam", by Edith Shiffert. Reprinted with permission of the author from her book *A Way to Find Out*, Raiyi Press, Kyoto, Japan. Copyright 1979. All rights reserved by Edith Shiffert.

Photograph acknowledgments: p. 5, Alan Cliburn, p. 7, Mark Morelli; p. 11, Northeastern University Office of Public Information; p. 14, Mark Morelli; p. 19, Philip Rothenberg; p. 20, Mark Morelli; p. 31, Photographs courtesy of Pennsylvania House—makers of fine American traditional furniture for over 50 years. Lewisburg, PA 17837; p. 40, Judie Bittinger; p. 44, NFB/Phototheque, photo by Bill Stanley; pp. 46, 47, 48, 51, National Aeronautics & Space Administration; p. 54, Northeastern University Office of Public Information; p. 56, Supreme Court of the U.S.; p. 58, Massachusetts General Hospital News Office; pp. 62, 64, Rick Hulbert; p. 69, National Archives; p. 70, Walter Collins O'Kane; p. 73, Arizona Office of Tourism photo; pp. 77, 79 State of Alaska Division of Tourism; p. 83, U.S. Department of the Interior Collection; p. 86, 98, The Museum of the American Indian, Heye Foundation; pp. 88, 94, Arizona Office of Tourism Photo; p. 92, National Archives; p. 99, New Mexico Economic Development and Tourist Department; pp. 103, 110, Vermont Travel Division; p. 116, USDA photo; p. 118, Ball Corporation; p. 123, Air Transport Association; pp. 126, 127, 130, Maine Department of Marine Resources; pp. 132, 133, 134, Hawaii Visitors Bureau Photos; p. 140, Claire Smith; pp. 145, 146, 147, 148, 156, TW Services Inc., Yellowstone National Park, WY.

Development of this textbook was partially funded by Japan Association of Language Teachers (JALT) research grants in 1980 and 1981

ISBN: 0-201-12244-8
CDEFGHIJ-TO-8987654

Table of Contents

Introduction

This book was developed to motivate you to read in English by providing you with cultural information about the United States. In order to improve your reading ability, each selection is followed by reading skills exercises. Exercises such as skimming, outlining, visualizing, and sequencing help you grasp concepts and gather information without resorting to your native language. The opening selections in this textbook, "Reading Without a Dictionary" and "Active Reading," will show you how to use the context and clues in order to understand the meaning even when you do not understand all the words. The writing exercises which follow most of the readings are designed to help you think about the material you have read, and develop your own ideas in writing.

The selections in "Poetry and Song" will help you with speech rhythms and make you more aware of word and sentence stress patterns. The pieces have been carefully chosen to reflect a variety of American values and interests.

As you improve your reading comprehension, we also encourage you to increase your reading speed. The number of words in each reading is indicated after the final paragraph. Whenever you read a selection, time yourself, then turn to the Reading Speed Chart on pages 158–160 to calculate the number of words you read per minute. Write your reading speed on the Time Record Chart and note how your speed improves as you progress through the lessons.

We wish to express our appreciation to all the contributors who gave their time to write materials, and in particular to Ms. Michiko Inoue, for her assistance in preparing this textbook. We would also like to thank Professor Shigeru Hasegawa, who used our experimental textbook and gave us suggestions for revision. We also extend our appreciation to Professors Bernard Susser, Howard Lazzarini, Junko Miyazaki, and Linda Donan for their suggestions, and to Professor Tsukasa Matsui, who helped with our preliminary research.

Kenji Kitao

I. Orientations

1
Reading
Without a Dictionary

When you read in English, you are likely to come across words or phrases that you don't understand. Looking these up in a dictionary can be very time-consuming and frustrating, however. This makes it difficult to enjoy reading, and it is impractical as well, if you have to
5 read very many pages at a time.

When you read in your native language, what do you do if you come across a word that you don't know? You may occasionally check with a dictionary, but most of the time you guess the meanings of unfamiliar words for the context. You can do the same when you read
10 in English.

Let's look at some examples. Even in the case of an easy word, you often understand the meaning only because of the context, because many words have more than one meaning. Take, for example, the word *race*. If you see it by itself, you don't know exactly what it means,
15 because it has more than one meaning. It can mean "a contest of speed," or it can mean "one of a number of divisions of human beings." But suppose you saw it in this sentence: "The horse won the race and the $10,000 prize." Which meaning do you think it has here? Since the words *horse, won,* and *prize* are associated with a contest
20 of speed rather than divisions of human beings, you could have guessed that in this sentence *race* means "a contest of speed."

You can sometimes guess the meanings of more difficult words in the same way. If you don't know the word "euphemism" and you read it in the sentence, *"Pass away* is a euphemism for *die,"* how do
25 you figure out what it means without looking in a dictionary? If you look at the other major words in the sentence—*pass away* and *die*— you see that they mean almost the same thing, but that *pass away* is an indirect and less harsh way of saying *die.* Therefore, a euphemism must be an indirect or less harsh way of saying something. You are
30 able to figure out the meaning of a word that you didn't know by looking for clues in the context.

Sometimes an author will tell you the meaning of an unfamiliar word, or restate the idea in a way that gives you a clue to the meaning of the unfamiliar word. The sentence, "She broke her tibia, a bone in
35 the lower part of her leg," is an example of the first technique. "A bone in the lower part of her leg" explains what the *tibia* is. Here you are able to understand the meaning of the word because the writer explains it. The sentence "His ideas are really half-baked; he just does not think them out well," is an example of a restatement of the idea.
40 The second half of the sentence restates the idea of the first, so *half-baked* means "not thought out well."

An author may also give an example or illustration of an unfamiliar word. In the sentence, "I was very apprehensive, as if I were waiting to see the dentist," the feeling being described is compared with the
45 common experience of waiting to see the dentist. How do you feel when waiting to see the dentist? You probably feel nervous about what might happen, and that's what *apprehensive* means.

Another kind of clue to look for is a word or phrase that is contrasted with the unfamiliar word. In the sentence, "When you
50 remember how shy he used to be, it's hard to believe how outgoing he is now," the word *shy*, which you probably know, is contrasted with the word *outgoing*, which may be unfamiliar. Since the opposite of *shy* is *friendly*, or *eager to mix socially*, you can guess what *outgoing* probably means.

55   You should keep in mind that it is not always necessary to understand the exact meaning of a word when you are reading. If you are able to get a general idea of the meaning of an unfamiliar word, that is sufficient for most types of reading.

These techniques may sound difficult and confusing, but if you 60 try using them, after a while you should find that your reading goes much more smoothly and is much more enjoyable. (718 words)

Vocabulary

1. <u>3</u>   **time-consuming:** *taking a lot of time*
2. <u>3</u>   **frustrating:** *making one feel discouraged*
3. <u>6</u>   **native language:** *the language one learns from birth*
4. <u>9</u>   **context:** *words and phrases which surround a certain word or phrase and help explain its meaning*
5. <u>25</u> **figure out:** *understand by thinking about*
6. <u>31</u> **clues:** *things that help find an answer to a question, difficulty, etc.*
7. <u>33</u> **restate:** *say again in different words*
8. <u>55</u> **keep in mind:** *remember*

Comprehension Questions

1. What are the problems in looking up all the words you don't know when you are reading in English?

2. When reading in your native language, what do you generally do if you come across a word that you don't know?

3. Is it possible to do the same thing in English?

4. How can you tell the exact meaning of an easy word that has more than one meaning?

5. Is the same technique possible with difficult words?

6. How else might you be able to figure out the meaning of an unfamiliar word?

7. What does the writer tell you to remember?

8. If you use these techniques, how will it affect your reading?

Application Exercise

A. The underlined words in the following sentences have more than one meaning. Choose the meaning that the word has in the context of the sentence. Circle the word(s) in the sentence that helped you.

   1. I deposited $200 in my savings account at the <u>bank</u>.
       a. land along the side of a river or lake
       b. a place where money is kept
       c. a mass of clouds, snow, or mud

   2. After a ten-mile hike, the soldiers returned to the army <u>base</u>.
       a. a military camp
       b. the part of an object on which it stands
       c. any of the four goals a runner must touch in order to make a run in baseball

   3. I <u>called</u> him on the phone and talked to him.
       a. shouted
       b. made a business or professional visit
       c. telephoned

B. Choose the definition that fits the underlined word or phrase, using other words in the sentence as clues.

   1. Many buildings were burned to the ground in the <u>conflagration</u> that followed the earthquake.
       a. a very large fire
       b. a sudden shaking of the earth's surface
       c. destruction

   2. The <u>torrential</u> rains caused floods that washed away bridges and buildings.
       a. light
       b. heavy
       c. unexpected

   3. He told me some <u>fairy tale</u> about where he got the money, but I think he was lying.
       a. a story that is difficult to believe
       b. a story about small, magical people
       c. a true story

4. She was <u>sanguine</u> about her chances of getting the job, so
    she was in a good mood when she went to the interview.
    a. discouraged; expecting the worst
    b. indifferent; neither hopeful nor discouraged
    c. eagerly hopeful; expecting the best

5. A well-known <u>philatelist</u> spoke to our club about stamp
    collecting.
    a. a person who collects stamps
    b. a person who is paid for speaking at clubs
    c. a club president

C. Circle the words or phrases in the following sentences that tell
    you the meaning of the underlined words or phrases.

    1. The teacher was from <u>Garden City</u>, a small town in Kansas.
    2. He couldn't work because of <u>sciatica</u>, severe pain in his leg
        and lower back.
    3. He telephoned at an <u>inopportune</u> moment, and it was incon-
        venient for me to stop and answer his questions.
    4. He's <u>susceptible to suggestion</u>, so it's easy to influence him.
    5. He's such a <u>miser</u> that it pains him to spend even a penny.

D. Choose the definition that fits the underlined word, using the
    example in the sentence as a clue.

    1. He is <u>unscrupulous</u> enough to cheat widows out of their life
        savings.
        a. careful about doing what is right
        b. a moral argument against something
        c. not caring about honesty or fairness in getting something

    2. The kitchen is <u>immaculate</u>—she must have spent hours
        cleaning it.
        a. very clean
        b. very dirty
        c. without fault

3. She's so <u>indolent</u> that it's easier for me to do a job myself than to try to get her to do it.
   a. hard-working
   b. allowing (herself) to enjoy (something)
   c. lazy

4. My stomach was <u>queasy</u>, as if I were seasick.
   a. empty
   b. full
   c. upset

5. He's really <u>phlegmatic</u>—you just never see him excited about anything.
   a. busy
   b. calm
   c. excitable

E. Choose the definition that fits the underlined word, using the contrast in the sentence as a clue.

1. He prattles on and on and never says anything important.
    a. talks about silly things
    b. talks about important matters
    c. talks a lot

2. I was hoping for an immediate decision, but the committee temporized.
    a. made a decision quickly
    b. delayed making a decision
    c. didn't make a decision

3. Though I met many obstacles, they didn't deter me.
    a. help (me) reach (my) goal
    b. affect (my) reaching (my) goal
    c. prevent (me) from reaching (my) goal

4. The two of them have opposite personalities—she's always serious, and he's a real clown.
    a. someone who acts foolish and tells jokes to make people laugh
    b. someone who prevents people from enjoying themselves
    c. someone who is always solemn and thoughtful

5. She doesn't have a reputation for generosity, but the gift she gave the church was munificent.
    a. small
    b. generous
    c. inspired by guilt

F. Using the techniques that you have learned, guess the meanings of the underlined words and phrases in the following sentences, and write down your guesses. Remember that you may not be able to guess the exact meanings, but you should be able to get a general idea.

1. We went through the house and collected old books, clothes, etc., and sold them at a rummage sale.

2. The material was <u>flimsy</u>, and it tore easily.
3. He bought a shirt, tie, and suit at a <u>haberdashery</u>.
4. He suffers from a <u>delusion</u>: he thinks he's Napoleon.
5. There is a great <u>disparity</u> between their ages—she's only nineteen, and he's almost sixty.
6. Judging from his ragged clothes, you'd think he was <u>indigent</u>, but he's actually quite rich.
7. Her calmness helped <u>dispel</u> my worries about the situation.
8. If you're going to be doing a lot of traveling, you shouldn't <u>encumber</u> yourself with a lot of luggage.
9. She was so <u>engrossed</u> in her work that she sometimes forgot to eat.
10. When I stood up to give my speech, I forgot what I had planned to say and had to <u>extemporize</u>.

Summary Exercise

Briefly explain each of the techniques that you have learned for guessing the meanings of words from their context.

1.

2.

3.

4.

2 Active Reading

Most of us have to read a certain amount of material for one reason or other: perhaps we are taking a course, perhaps we need to read something for work, perhaps we are giving a talk on an outside interest to a group or club. All too often we approach such an assignment
5 with the idea of reading a certain number of pages, or starting at the beginning and reading page by page until we have completed the reading. While this approach does get the reading over with, it does not encourage you think about what you are reading—to participate actively.

10   People who enjoy reading have learned to look for clues or key ideas as they read. They often do this without realizing it, but it is part of what makes reading fun. If you have never tried this technique, you might want to see how it works. In some ways it's like taking a trip someplace you've never been. You wouldn't just start off and
15 hope you were going in the right direction; you would probably check a road map carefully to see the direction you want to go, the types of roads, the location of towns or other special points. It's the same with

reading. If you have some idea of what is included in the material and how it is presented, you will get more out of your reading and enjoy
20 it more. You can do this by looking over the reading briefly in a methodical way to see the main points of the chapter or article.

First, read the opening paragraph or two. This introductory material will acquaint you with the main thought that the author will discuss. Then read the first sentences of the next few paragraphs. These
25 sentences will probably give you a general idea of the content. Then read the final paragraph or two, which will give you a summary of the material covered. You should note anything the author has used to add emphasis: headings, bold-face type, italics, graphs, pictures, and questions at the end of the chapter. This preview of your reading
30 should be done very quickly.

Second, re-read the whole assignment more thoroughly. The speed and emphasis of this second reading will depend upon the information and direction you gained from your preview of the material. For example, you will often be able to judge the importance of a
35 paragraph by its first, or topic, sentence. If it seems important, read it carefully. If, on the basis of your first reading, the paragraph does not seem so important, it is probably sufficient to skim it, but do not skip it entirely.

You will need to adapt your approach to fit the writing style of
40 the author. In some books various sections have topics set in bold-face type or set out in the margins. Use these as guides to the content. Questions at the end of the chapter can give you an idea of what is contained in that chapter.

As you read, try to relate this assignment to what you already
45 know about the topic. Is it new material? Does it differ from your earlier thinking on the subject? Ask yourself these simple questions as you move along: why? what? who? when? where? how? This approach can help you concentrate on the assignment, because as you ask questions you are taking an active role as a reader.
50 With such a systematic approach you will be able to direct your attention and concentration toward understanding the material more completely. The better your initial understanding of your reading, the easier it will be to retain and integrate the information. You will not be wasting your time; you will be making more efficient use of the
55 time you have. You may also find that reading has become more fun than work! (641 words)

Vocabulary

1. <u>4</u>   **assignment:** *work given*
2. <u>21</u> **methodical:** *using an ordered system*
3. <u>22</u> **paragraph:** *division of a written or printed piece which deals with one central idea, and is made up of one or more sentences: the first word of the paragraph often begins a few spaces further to the right than the remaining material*
4. <u>28</u> **headings:** *the words written as a title at the top of a piece of writing or at the top of each part of it*
5. <u>28</u> **bold-face type:** *thick black letters*
6. <u>28</u> **italics:** *a style of printing with sloping letters*
7. <u>28</u> **graphs:** *drawings that show how values are related to one another*
8. <u>29</u> **preview:** *looking over quickly before beginning to read thoroughly*
9. <u>35</u> **topic sentence:** *sentence containing the main idea*
10. <u>37</u> **skim:** *look over quickly for the main ideas*
11. <u>53</u> **integrate:** *join together so as to form a whole*

Organization Exercise

Put the following statements in the order of the story.

a. Systematic reading will help to improve reading comprehension.
b. When you read, it helps if you know what is included and how it is presented.
c. Try to make connections between what you are reading and what you already know.
d. Judging by the topic sentence, decide whether you should read a paragraph thoroughly.
e. Reading an article straight through is not the most effective method of reading.
f. Your approach to reading your assignment will need to be adapted to fit the format of the article.
g. First preview your assignment quickly.

1	2	3	4	5	6	7

Comprehension and Combination Exercise

Choose three correct statements in each group and combine them into one sentence, as in the following example:

When you have to read a certain amount of material,
a. you can read the assignment straight through
b. this is an effective method of reading
c. this is not the most effective method of reading
d. it does not encourage you to read actively
e. it allows you to enjoy your reading

Combining (a), (c), and (d) gives this sentence:

When you have to read a certain amount of material, you can read the assignment straight through, but this is not the most effective method of reading because it does not encourage you to read actively.

1. In previewing your assignment,
    a. read the first couple of paragraphs
    b. read the last sentence of each paragraph
    c. read the last few paragraphs
    d. pay attention to headings, bold type, italics, graphs, pictures, etc.
    e. skip any part which is boring
    f. spend as much time as you want in previewing

2. In the second reading,
   a. read the assignment more thoroughly
   b. read important paragraphs carefully
   c. judge how important each paragraph is from its length
   d. skim unimportant paragraphs rapidly
   e. skip any paragraphs whose topic sentences do not seem important
   f. read as fast as you can

_____

_____

3. When you read,
   a. you need to know the writing style of the author
   b. try to connect what you are reading with what you already know
   c. do not read systematically
   d. take an active role, asking questions such as why, what, where, when, and how
   e. ask your teacher questions
   f. you waste your time if you use the systematic approach

_____

_____

Comprehension Questions

1. How can you get an idea of what is included in the material and how it is arranged?

2. In previewing a new article, which paragraphs do you read carefully?

3. How fast should you preview the article?

4. In the second reading, which sentences do you pay attention to?

5. Which paragraphs do you skim rapidly?

Vocabulary Exercises

A. For each of these words find the part of speech asked for:

1. **approach** -noun _____
2. **assignment** -verb _____
3. **completed** -noun _____
4. **encourage** -noun _____
5. **participate** -noun _____
6. **methodical** -noun _____
7. **introductory** -noun _____
8. **acquaint** -noun _____
9. **summary** -verb _____
10. **quickly** -adjective _____
11. **entirely** -noun _____
12. **adapt** -noun _____
13. **need** -noun _____
14. **contained** -noun _____

15. **relate** -noun _____
16. **differ** -adjective _____
17. **concentrate** -noun _____
18. **attention** -adjective _____
19. **retain** -noun _____
20. **integrate** -noun _____

B. What are the antonyms of these words?

1. actively _____
2. author _____
3. gained _____
4. earlier _____
5. simple _____
6. initial _____
7. efficient _____

C. Fill in the blank with a form of a word from the main text.

1. Our English teacher gives us a lot of _____ every week.

2. You should not just sit in class and listen to your classmates. Your active _____ in the class is required.

3. We explored the area to find a suitable _____ for our camp.

4. _____ reading of homework assignments will improve your reading comprehension.

5. The last _____ will give you a summary of the whole article.

6. The _____ of *The Old Man and the Sea* is Ernest Hemingway.

7. If you read the _____ before reading an article; you will have an idea of what the article is about.

8. When you go to a movie theater, you see a _____ of the next movie.

9. A _____ investigation will show that the man was murdered.

10. We have to _____ ourselves to our environment.

11. If necessary, you may write in the _____ of this book.

12. What does this bottle _____?

13. The grade you receive in a class is _____ to how hard you study.

14. I cannot _____ on just one thing, because I am interested in so many things.

15. Although he is very old, he still _____ a lot of vitality.

16. When you read, try to _____ what you are reading with what you already know.

17. Our teacher has adopted _____ methods of teaching.

Summary Exercise

1. What is the main thought the author discusses in this article? (Read the first two paragraphs.)

2. Pick out topic sentences in the third, fourth, fifth, and sixth paragraphs.

3. Write a summary of this article. (Read the last paragraph.)

4. Choose a textbook to analyze. Pick out headings, bold type, italics, graphs, etc., which the author has used to add emphasis, if any.

NOW APPLY THESE SIMPLE STRATEGIES TO THE NEXT TWO READINGS.

3
The American Concept of Time

People of different cultures have differing views of time, its qualities, and its uses. The American concept of time is largely shared with northern Europeans, and though there are regional and personal variations among Americans, some generalizations can be made.

5   Americans consider time a commodity, a tangible thing. This can be demonstrated in the words that Americans use in describing what they do with time. Time can be bought or sold, saved or spent. People can waste time, or lose it, and then they can make up for its loss.

Americans usually make appointments with only one person at a 10 time. American businesspeople find it disconcerting, in a country where this is not the practice, to arrive for a business appointment and discover that the person they are meeting is carrying on business with several other people at the same time.

Americans tend to distinguish whether or not a person is engaged 15 in an activity. They don't consider "just sitting" and thinking or meditating to be "doing anything." One must be actively involved in writing, talking, listening, playing a game, etc., to be considered as "doing something." Thus remarks such as, "You didn't seem to be doing anything, so I thought I'd stop in and talk," are commonly 20 made.

Americans don't question the view that time should be planned and future events fitted into a schedule. The past is not to be dwelled on too much. The future is not very far ahead. People generally plan one or two years ahead—usually not more than five. Beyond that, the 25 future doesn't seem too real. However, promises to meet deadlines are taken seriously, and therefore there are penalties for failing to keep such promises.

The time that it takes to do anything is quantified. There are two main ways of quantifying time—formally and informally. Formal quan- 30 tities of time are to be taken literally. A year has 365 days, an hour has sixty minutes, etc. For example, a person who says, "I'll be there in

forty-five minutes," means that, barring unforeseen circumstances, s/he will arrive in about forty-five minutes and probably not more than a few minutes earlier or later. If a person says, "I lived in Europe for
35 six months," s/he lived in Europe for about six months, and probably not over a month more or less. Although some of the vocabulary for informal time is the same as for formal time (seconds, minutes, hours, years), the meanings depend on the context and on the individual who is speaking. "I'll be there in a second," can mean any time up to
40 several minutes. "This is going to take years," can refer to a length of

time from minutes to actual years. Other vocabulary words used in informal time include "later," "soon," and "a while."

Duration of time sometimes carries a message with it. For example, promptness for a business appointment is important. Lateness is a
45 sign of disrespect, the amount of disrespect being correlated to the number of minutes late. To be a few minutes early shows deference to the person you are to meet. Being up to five minutes late is not significant in most cases. Being from five to fifteen minutes late requires a short, informal apology. Being more than forty-five minutes
50 late requires a sincere apology and an explanation of the circumstances that delayed you and prevented you from calling and notifying the person. To cite another example of the messages that duration of time can give, the statements, "He spent an hour with the President," and "Ms. Bradley could only give us ten minutes of her time," also convey
55 messages about the importance of the business. If the President spends an hour with someone, it is undoubtedly on an important matter. On the other hand, if Ms. Bradley could only spare ten minutes, she probably did not consider the matter to be of great importance.

Time of day can also convey messages related to importance. For
60 example, one does not usually call people early in the morning (when they are getting ready for school or work) or later than ten o'clock at night except on a matter of utmost importance. In fact, one does not usually call during normal sleeping hours except for life and death concerns.

65 Time of arrival is important in social situations. For example, if you are invited to an American home for dinner and are told, "We'll be eating at 6:00," you are expected to arrive about ten minutes early. If you are told, "Please come at 6:00," you are expected at 6:00— certainly not more than a few minutes later, because the meal will be
70 prepared so that it can be served at a certain time. However, the time of arrival, especially in social situations, is much more loosely given on the West Coast. If you are asked to arrive at 6:00, you are not expected much before 6:30.

There are, of course, exceptions to these rules about time. Young
75 people tend to be more casual about deadlines, appointments, etc., than older people. People from different countries living in the United States may have different rules from the general population, especially if they live and work in a community with other people of similar background. (878 words)

Vocabulary

1. T   **concept:** *general idea, thought, or understanding*
2. 4   **generalizations:** *general statements or opinions resulting from the consideration of particular facts*
3. 5   **commodity:** *useful thing, especially an article of trade*
4. 5   **tangible:** *able to be touched; treated as a material object*
5. 10 **disconcerting:** *causing one to feel uncomfortable*
6. 16 **meditating:** *thinking seriously or deeply*
7. 18 **remarks:** *written or spoken statements*
8. 22 **dwelled on:** *thought, spoken, or written about a great deal*
9. 25 **deadlines:** *times before which something must be done*
10. 28 **quantified:** *measured*
11. 30 **literally:** *according to the exact meaning of the words*
12. 32 **unforeseen:** *unexpected*
13. 38 **context:** *setting in which a word, phrase, etc., is used, often helping to explain the meaning*
14. 43 **duration:** *the time during which something exists or lasts*
15. 45 **being correlated:** *having a relationship*
16. 50 **sincere apology:** *apology which the hearer believes the apologizer really means*
17. 52 **cite:** *mention; quote*
18. 54 **Ms.:** *title for a woman that does not indicate whether or not she is married (contrast with Mrs./Miss)*
19. 62 **utmost:** *of the greatest degree*

Skimming Exercise

1. According to the second paragraph, what is one characteristic of the American attitude toward time?

2. According to the fourth paragraph, do Americans consider sitting and thinking as "doing something?"

3. According to the seventh paragraph, what is lateness a sign of?

4. According to the last paragraph, do all Americans have the same concept of time?

True/False/Not enough information (?)

If the statement is false, rewrite it so that it is true.

T F ?   1. The American concept of time is similar to the northern European concept of time.

T F ?   2. Americans do not think of time as being tangible.

T F ?   3. An American would be pleased to arrive at a business appointment and find that other people had appointments at the same time.

T F ?   4. According to the American way of thinking, a person who is "just sitting" is doing something.

T F ?   5. Americans usually don't plan more than six months ahead.

T F ?   6. "Later" and "soon" are vocabulary words used in talking about informal time.

T F ?   7. In informal time, a year has 365 days.

T F ?   8. In formal time, a minute has fifty seconds.

T F ?   9. If a person says, "I talked to my friend on the phone for fifteen minutes," s/he is probably using formal time.

T F ?   10. It is insulting to be more than two minutes late for a business appointment in the United States.

T F ?   11. You do not need to apologize for being late for a business appointment in the United States unless you are over a half hour late.

T F ?   12. If you want to ask an American classmate a question about homework, you should call before ten in the evening.

T F ? 13. If you are asked to come to an American home for dinner at 7:00, you should arrive at 6:30.

T F ? 14. People in America all have the same rules for the use of time.

Vocabulary Exercises

Change the following words according to the directions.

A. Parts of Speech

1.	**northern**	-noun	_____
2.	**tangible**	-noun	_____
3.	**demonstrated**	-noun	_____
4.	**meditating**	-noun	_____
5.	**question**	-noun	_____
6.	**penalties**	-verb	_____
7.	**quantified**	-noun	_____
8.	**probably**	-adjective	_____
9.	**promptness**	-adverb	_____
10.	**deference**	-verb	_____
11.	**significant**	-noun	_____
12.	**requires**	-noun	_____
13.	**apology**	-verb	_____
14.	**statements**	-verb	_____
15.	**invited**	-noun	_____
16.	**expected**	-noun	_____

B. What is a synonym for each of these words?

1. **views**   _____
2. **distinguish** _____
3. **generally**   _____

C.   What is an antonym for each of these words?

  1. **northern**   _____

  2. **unforeseen**   _____

  3. **normal**   _____

  4. **arrival**   _____

Writing Exercise

The fact that Americans consider time to have tangible qualities can be demonstrated by the verbs that they use in connection with it. For example, if you pay someone to do a job, you are *buying* their time, as well as their knowledge, abilities, etc. If it takes you three hours to do a job that you should be able to finish in one hour, you are probably *wasting* time.

Give examples of incidents during the past month when you have done four of the following:

1.   Sold time:

2.   Made up time:

3.   Lost time:

4.   Wasted time:

5.   Saved time:

6.   Spent time:

Summary Exercise

  1.   Summarize each paragraph in one sentence.

  2.   Compare your summary sentences with other students' sentences. Revise your sentences, if you wish.

  3.   Using the summary sentences as a basis, write a brief summary of the main text.

4
The American Concept of Space

People carry within themselves concepts of the space around them,
including a sense of territorial boundaries and feelings about what
areas are appropriate for different types of activities and what degrees
of distance between people are appropriate in various interpersonal
5 situations. These concepts vary according to culture, situation, and
individual differences. Cultural variations can cause misunderstandings
when people of different cultures interact. Because of the subconscious
nature of concepts about space, the people involved often do not
understand exactly why there is a conflict.

10   It is difficult to make general statements about American culture,
since many very different groups make up this culture. These groups
have come from all over the world, bringing with them their own ways
of dealing with interactions. Besides these differences, there are also
very wide differences in social patterns in the geographical sections
15 of the United States. The South is not exactly like the Northeast in its
social interactions, for example. Nevertheless, there are some patterns
which can be discussed.

Territoriality is a very strong concept in American culture. Remov-
ing boundary markers or trespassing on private property are acts that
20 are punishable by law. In fact, some Americans would even consider
it their right to shoot and kill someone that they found robbing their
house. To enter someone else's house without knocking and receiving
permission to enter is a very serious breach of courtesy (except in the
case of very close friends or relatives).

25   Territoriality also exists within American homes. The kitchen is
usually considered the wife's territory, while the workshop, if there is
one, is the husband's. Some family members have their "own" chairs
in the living room. People usually sit at the same places at the table
for every meal. In addition, children often have their own bedrooms.
30 Even if siblings share a bedroom, the room is generally divided into
territories by an invisible, but very real, line.

Physical privacy is considered important in America. When a person wants privacy, he or she will usually go into a room that can be considered his or her territory and close the door. In contrast, in
35 some cultures a person who wants privacy will not necessarily go into a room alone but will instead merely indicate by mannerisms a desire not to be disturbed. People who share this culture are familiar with these mannerisms, but often Americans, accustomed to guaranteeing privacy with physical barriers, do not recognize these signs, and this
40 can be a point of conflict.

American homes—in common with most Western-style dwellings—are organized spatially, with different functions being assigned to different rooms. There are rooms for food preparation, eating, socializing, sleeping, and so on. Usually one does not, for example,
45 eat in a room intended for sleeping. Rooms are named for their function—living room, bedroom, dining room, etc. As a general rule, people move from room to room or from one part of a room to another as activities change, rather than moving the articles associated with the activity.

50   Use of space in interpersonal relationships is another aspect of
concepts of space that often causes misunderstanding between people
of different cultures. The distance maintained between people in a
given situation depends on the culture, the nature of the relationship
and of the transaction, the moods of the individuals at the time, and/
55 or individual differences. Maintenance of distance is largely subconscious. It is difficult to specify why, in a given situation, one might
feel that another person is too far away, too close, or at a comfortable
distance.

Observers have described four zones of interpersonal distance:
60 intimate, personal, social, and public. The following is a description
of these distance zones as they are used by most Americans. Intimate
distance is from contact to 18 inches. It is the distance used for
comforting, wrestling, sex, sharing secrets, and so on. If the voice is
used, its volume is low. Physical contact is easily made. This distance
65 is not generally considered proper for use between adults in public,
except in situations, such as in an elevator, where it is unavoidable.
In these types of situations, Americans are very uncomfortable.

Personal distance ranges from 18 inches to four feet. It is used
between close friends or family members for discussions of personal
70 interest. Touching is possible, but not unavoidable. The volume of
the voice is moderate.

Social distance ranges from four to twelve feet, and it is used for
impersonal transactions. People who work together or who are attending a casual social gathering use the close end (four to seven feet)
75 of this zone. More formal business and social transactions are carried
on in the far phase. The volume of the voice is noticeably louder than
for the personal distance zone, and touching is not possible without
leaning forward.

The public distance zone is twelve feet or more. It is used for
80 public occasions. The voice must be raised in order to be heard, and
speech is in a rather formal style.

The distances described here are, of course, applicable only to
Americans, and even so, do not apply to every subculture within the
United States. The distance zones of other cultures vary widely. For
85 example, what is considered intimate distance by an American would
be considered social distance by people of some other nationalities,
such as Arabs or Italians. This can result in some rather amusing
situations, such as one an Italian-American described, when his uncle,
visiting from Italy, virtually chased an American-born nephew around
90 the room in order to get within what the uncle considered correct
social distance.

As we have seen, not everyone has the same concepts of space.
When dealing with people of other cultures, it is important to have
some understanding of their concepts of space. Sources of conflict
95 will be more easily recognized and solutions more easily found.
(976 words)

Vocabulary

1. __T__ **concept:** *general idea, thought, or understanding*
2. __2__ **territorial:** *related to a particular area considered to belong to somebody or something*
3. __2__ **boundaries:** *borders; dividing lines between surfaces or spaces*
4. __4__ **interpersonal:** *being related to or concerning relations between persons*
5. __7__ **interact:** *have an effect on each other*
6. __7__ **subconscious:** *(thoughts, feelings, etc.) not fully known to the mind*
7. __19__ **markers:** *objects that mark a place*
8. __19__ **trespassing:** *going onto privately-owned land without permission*
9. __23__ **breach of courtesy:** *failure to observe good manners*
10. __26__ **workshop:** *place where things are made or repaired*
11. __30__ **siblings:** *brothers and sisters*
12. __36__ **mannerisms:** *particular ways of behaving, speaking, etc.*

13. <u>42</u> **spatially:** *related to space*
14. <u>44</u> **socializing:** *spending time with others in a friendly way*
15. <u>54</u> **transaction:** *business, social relationships, etc., that are carried on between people*
16. <u>55</u> **maintenance:** *keeping*
17. <u>56</u> **specify:** *state exactly*
18. <u>63</u> **wrestling:** *fighting by holding and throwing the opponent's body*
19. <u>71</u> **moderate:** *of middle degree; neither loud nor soft*
20. <u>74</u> **gathering:** *meeting*
21. <u>78</u> **leaning:** *bending forward, usually from the waist*
22. <u>82</u> **applicable:** *able to be directly related*
23. <u>83</u> **subculture:** *group of persons within a society that has cultural patterns different from the larger society*
24. <u>88</u> **Italian-American:** *American of Italian origin*
25. <u>89</u> **virtually:** *almost; very nearly*
26. <u>89</u> **chased:** *followed rapidly in order to catch*
27. <u>95</u> **solutions:** *ways of solving a problem*

Skimming Exercise

1. According to the first paragraph, what concepts do people carry inside themselves?

2. According to the third paragraph, what is a very strong concept in American culture?

3. What, according to paragraph 4, is a place where territoriality exists?

4. Is privacy considered important, according to paragraph 5?

5. What are the four zones of interpersonal distance listed and described in the eighth paragraph?

6. Are the distances described here the same for people all over the world? (See paragraph 12)

7. According to the last paragraph, what is important when dealing with people of other cultures?

True/False/Not enough information (?)

If the statement is false, rewrite it so that it is true.

T F ?   1. Everyone has the same concept of space.

T F ?   2. People from different cultures don't always understand
            why they have conflicts over use of space.

T F ?   3. In the United States, a person making a delivery will
            open the door of a house without knocking in order to
            leave a package.

T F ?   4. Americans indicate by their mannerisms that they do
            not want to be disturbed.

T F ?   5. Americans usually eat and prepare food in the same
            room.

T F ?   6. The type of relationship that two people have affects
            how far apart they stand or sit.

T F ?   7. Most people can explain why they maintain a certain
            distance in a given situation.

T F ?   8. Personal distance is usually used between co-workers.

T F ?   9. All Americans make use of the same distances zones.

T F ? 10. An understanding of the concepts of space that people
            of different cultures have will help reduce conflict.

Comprehension Questions

1. Why don't people understand why they have conflicts related to
    the use of space?

2. Give four examples of territoriality in American culture.

3. How do Americans indicate that they want to be alone?

4. How are Western-style homes spatially organized?

5. In which zone of interpersonal distance is touching impossible?

6. In which zone is the voice softest?

7. How do the distance zones of Americans and Italians differ?

Vocabulary Exercise

The following are definitions of words or phrases that appear in this article. They are arranged in order and according to paragraph. Find the word or phrase that is defined and write it in the appropriate blank.

Paragraph 1

1. _____: general ideas, thoughts, or understandings

2. _____: steps or stages in a set of steps, from the nearest to the most distant

3. _____: different types of the same thing

4. _____: the clash of opposite ideas or beliefs

Paragraph 3

5. _____: morally just or lawful claim

6. _____: agreement; consent

Paragraph 4

7. _____: the main room in a house where people can do things together

8. _____: usually

9. _____: not able to be seen due to nature or size

Paragraph 5

10. _____: the state of being away from the presence or notice of others

Paragraph 6

11. _____: special purposes

12. _____: spending time with others in a friendly way

Paragraph 7

13. _____: a particular side of something that has many sides

Paragraph 8

14. _____: divisions or areas marked off from others by particular qualities

15. _____: loudness of sound

Paragraph 9

16. _____: varies (between limits)

Paragraph 10

17. _____: not showing or including one's feelings

Paragraph 11

18. _____: made louder

Paragraph 12

19. _____: thought of as

20. _____: funny

Cloze Exercise

Scholars have described four interpersonal distance zones: intimate, personal, 1_____, and public. From 2_____ to 18 inches is intimate. At this 3_____, Americans comfort each other, 4_____, have sex, share 5_____, etc. Intimate distance is not usually thought to be 6_____ for adults in most 7_____ situations, except where crowding 8_____ unavoidable, such as in an 9_____. At such times, Americans feel very 10_____.

From 11_____ inches to four 12_____ is personal distance. Close friends or 13_____ members use it for personal 14_____. Touching is possible, but can be 15_____.

Culture Exercise

A. In the following situations, which of the four distance zones are *Americans* most likely to use? Circle the number.

1 = intimate   2 = personal   3 = social   4 = public

1 2 3 4   1. speaking before a large group

1 2 3 4   2. discussing a problem with a close friend

1 2 3 4   3. asking directions of a stranger

1 2 3 4   4. .listening to a speech by a famous scientist

1 2 3 4   5. telling a secret

1 2 3 4   6. asking a question of a teacher

1 2 3 4   7. talking to an acquaintance at a party

1 2 3 4   8. comforting someone who is crying

B. In the following situations, which of the four distance zones are
the people of your culture most likely to use?

1 = intimate   2 = personal   3 = social   4 = public

1 2 3 4   1. speaking before a large group

1 2 3 4   2. discussing a problem with a close friend

1 2 3 4   3. asking directions of a stranger

1 2 3 4   4. listening to a speech by a famous scientist

1 2 3 4   5. telling a secret

1 2 3 4   6. asking a question of a teacher

1 2 3 4   7. talking to an acquaintance at a party

1 2 3 4   8. comforting someone who is crying

C. Discuss the difference and similarities found in A and B.

Further Study

Using the information in this reading, reflect on the zones of interpersonal distance in your culture and confirm your ideas by looking
up information in books about psychology or interpersonal commu-
nication. How do the zones differ from the ones described here? Are
the same zones used in the same situations?

II. People and Things

5 The Paper Bag

The brown paper bag has just become a hundred years old, and we should celebrate.

That paper grocery bag is a symbol of many good things. We can bring it home from the food store full of meat and vegetables, and it
5 becomes an image of prosperity; it brings thoughts of shiny apples, dry cereal, clean, warm kitchens—America. When we fold the bag flat and store it under the kitchen sink it becomes an image of thrift, of saving everything to use again.

Years ago paper bags were made by hand by boys working for
10 grocers. In 1851, a Pennsylvania school teacher invented a machine to make the bags, but his bags did not stand upright and could not be folded and stored flat. Then the first modern bag was produced; it had a flat rectangular bottom and pleated sides. And in 1910, manu- facturers began producing bags from a tough new kind of paper called
15 *kraft* (a German word meaning 'strength').

Ever since then, the brown paper grocery bag has flourished. Every American home has a stack of neatly folded large bags which came home full of groceries and now wait for their next use. It's a large stack, too, because many shoppers insist on "double bagging"
20 to be sure their groceries aren't too heavy for the bag. The bags will have many uses. They will take out trash and garbage; they will be turned into children's costumes; they will wrap packages; they will be cut up for book covers. There's no end to the things these bags can do.

25 There really are a lot of brown bags around. In 1982, the nation's 26,680 supermarkets bought about 25 billion grocery sacks made from good, honest kraft paper. Some, however, predict hard times ahead. A forest products expert says the paper bag will eventually give way to a polyethylene one, just the way the glass milk bottle and the paper
30 cup has. He says the plastic bags are almost cheap enough to replace paper bags now. For the moment, however, customers still prefer paper for their groceries. As one market manager says, "Maybe plastic is the wave of the future, but not to my customers. They all feel you can't put much in the plastic shopping bags and that they rip. I'd have
35 a hard time selling plastic to them instead of paper." (395 words)

Vocabulary

1. <u>5</u> **shiny:** *bright; brightly polished*
2. <u>6</u> **dry cereal:** *cornflakes, etc., eaten with milk and sugar for breakfast*
3. <u>7</u> **sink:** *large basin in a kitchen for washing pots, vegetables, etc.*
4. <u>7</u> **thrift:** *wise, economical management of money*
5. <u>13</u> **rectangular:** *having a shape with two long sides, two shorter sides, and four 90 degree corners*
6. <u>13</u> **pleated:** *having folds; folded*
7. <u>17</u> **stack:** *neat pile*
8. <u>19</u> **double bagging:** *putting one bag inside another before putting in groceries*
9. <u>21</u> **trash:** *worthless things to be thrown away*
10. <u>21</u> **garbage:** *useless food scraps to be thrown away*
11. <u>23</u> **cut up:** *cut into pieces*
12. <u>25</u> **around:** *everywhere*
13. <u>27</u> **honest:** *reliable*
14. <u>28</u> **give way to:** *be replaced by; be given up for*
15. <u>29</u> **polyethelene:** *kind of plastic (see plastic below)*
16. <u>30</u> **plastic:** *strong, light, man-made chemical material which can be manufactured in many shapes for many different uses*
17. <u>33</u> **wave of the future:** *the way things will be in the future*
18. <u>35</u> **selling:** *persuading (someone) to accept a new product, idea, etc.*

True/False/Not enough information (?)

If a statement is false, rewrite it so that it is true.

T F ? 1. We should celebrate the 100th birthday of the brown paper bag because it is a symbol of many good things.

T F ? 2. Years ago, paper bags were made by hand by grocers.

T F ? 3. Grocers did not use the first paper bags made by machine.

T F ? 4. The first modern bag had flat rectangular sides and a pleated bottom.

T F ? 5. Because of "double bagging," many American homes have a large stack of folded paper bags.

T F ? 6. There are only five things paper bags can be used for.

T F ? 7. 25 billion Americans bought grocery sacks in 1982.

T F ? 8. Most milk bottles and paper cups are now made of plastic.

T F ? 9. Plastic bags are cheap enough to replace paper bags.

T F ? 10. Customers think plastic is the wave of the future.

Comprehension Questions

1. How long have brown paper bags been in use?

2. Why does the writer think the brown paper bag is a symbol of prosperity?

3. What was wrong with the first bags made by machine?

4. In this essay, how many examples of uses does the writer give for paper bags?

5. Do customers now prefer plastic bags for their groceries? Why or why not?

Reference Exercise

Write the word or phrases that the following words refer to.

1. <u>4</u>   **it:**
2. <u>7</u>   **it:**
3. <u>11</u> **his:**
4. <u>16</u> **then:**
5. <u>18</u> **their:**
6. <u>22</u> **they:**
7. <u>29</u> **one:**
8. <u>33</u> **they:**
9. <u>34</u> **they:**
10. <u>35</u> **them:**

Worker at a bag-making machine

Cloze Exercise

Write the correct words or phrases in the blanks.

In the United States, brown paper bags are now a hundred
1_____ 2_____. Years ago, they were
made 3_____ 4_____. Bags made by ma-
chine from a strong paper called 5_____ were first produced in 1910. Ever 6_____ 7_____, Americans have been using brown paper bags to bring 8_____
home from the 9_____ 10_____. After that,
they use the bags to take out 11_____ and garbage. The
bags are also 12_____ into children's costumes, wrapping
paper, and book covers.

According 13_____ a forest products 14_____,
15_____ will be used for bags instead of paper. Already,
milk bottles and 16_____ cups have been 17_____
by plastic ones.

Discussion Questions

1. What are the ways to bring things home from the store? Are paper bags used a great deal in your culture? If not, what is used?

2. Is there a common material in your culture which has many uses, the way the paper bag does in the U.S.? If so, what are the uses?

3. Do you think it is wasteful to use so much paper and throw it away? Is the American society generally wasteful? In what ways is your society wasteful or not wasteful?

Writing Exercise

Choose some product of your own culture which everyone uses. Write several paragraphs about it. You can tell about its history, how many people use it, describe the product itself, give your opinion of it, and predict its future use.

6 The Man on the Moon

Fifty years ago American children played "Cowboys and Indians," and planned elaborate fantasies about living on a ranch when they grew up. Westerns were the most popular kind of escape literature for young people and for adults, too. But that has all changed, and one
5 of the people who helped make that change is Neil Armstrong, the American astronaut who was the first person to set foot on the moon. Now children play space games and plan imaginary trips through space. They speak of going to the moon and the planets so casually that you might think there were regularly scheduled passenger flights.
10 And space travel science fiction has replaced the cowboy story as the way to imagine oneself in another world.

Astronaut Edwin Aldrin, Jr., and the Eagle

Neil Armstrong was from the Midwest, and went to Purdue University in Indiana to become an engineer. After three years as a Navy pilot, he became a civilian test pilot flying rocket airplanes. This
15 background qualified him when astronauts were being chosen for the Apollo moon space program, as the candidates had to be test pilots and also have a degree in engineering or science.

Astronaut Neil Armstrong, Apollo 11
Commander

The romantic view of space travel only sees the exciting flights, but Armstrong had to go through a long training program to prepare
20 himself for the space project. In fact, much of Armstrong's time was spent in school. He studied scientific subjects related to the space flights, such as computer theory and flight mechanics. He also went through a series of exercises to learn how to work under the conditions of weightlessness which he would later encounter in space travel. To
25 experience the lack of gravity, he rode in a large airplane which was flown through a series of curving climbs and dives. For about thirty seconds of each curve he floated weightlessly, as he later would in space. He also practiced moon landings inside a simulator; through the window he was shown the simulated moon surface as he learned
30 to bring his spacecraft down on the moon. The astronauts were trained to carefully examine the landing surface of the moon before they set

the rocket down. If the spacecraft became damaged during the landing and it could not be repaired, the astronauts would be stranded on the moon. He also had to learn how to escape from the spacecraft after 35 it returned to earth and landed, in case there were mechanical problems. Finally Armstrong went through a two-year flight training program to prepare for the scientific tasks of the specific flight he was to go on. This included studying the surface of the moon, and studying geology in order to learn how to select rock samples on the moon.

40   On July 20, 1969, astronaut Neil Armstrong stepped out of the Eagle, the small rocket that had carried the astronauts from their spacecraft Apollo 11 down to the surface of the moon. The landing was televised to the earth and watched by millions around the world. For two hours Armstrong and his fellow astronaut, Edwin Aldrin, Jr., 45 explored the surface of the moon. They wore special backpacks outside the spacecraft which had all the equipment necessary to keep them alive in the airless environment of the moon. They did not find it difficult to move around, and quickly became used to the gravity of the moon which is only one-sixth as strong as that of the earth.

Setting up experiments on the moon

50   They collected rock samples and set up scientific experiments. They left instruments on the moon to detect earthquakelike vibrations. They also set up a reflector for a laser beam (an extremely intense

beam of light). This was later used to accurately measure the distance
to the moon by measuring the time it took for light to go to the moon
55 and return to earth. When the astronauts took off from the moon they
left behind a plaque: "Here men from the planet earth first set foot
upon the moon. We came in peace for all mankind."

As in a science fiction story, there was a great deal of concern
about possible dangerous germs that might be brought back from the
60 moon. So when the astronauts returned to earth, they—and their
equipment—and all the material from the moon—were scrubbed with
disinfectant. Then they were isolated for more than two weeks to see
if anything happened. Fortunately, no harmful material was found.

Armstrong worked in the space program until 1971, when he
65 became a professor at the University of Cincinnati in Ohio. People all
over the world treasure the memory of the blurry televised picture,
and the words which Armstrong said as he took that historic first step
onto the moon: "That's one small step for a man, one giant leap for
mankind."

70 That was an important step in the exploration of space which has
continued to the present attempts to establish permanent space stations
with shuttle spacecraft which will go back and forth to the earth.
Scientists are searching for the answers to many questions about the
universe, and the human desire to cross the frontier of the unknown
75 will keep sending astronauts into space. Once the search led into the
unknown world beyond the oceans; now it leads into boundless space.
(873 words)

Vocabulary

1. <u>1</u> **cowboys:** *people who work with cattle in the American West, usually on horseback*
2. <u>1</u> **"Cowboys and Indians":** *a game in which children pretend to be cowboys and Indians in the American West during the last century*
3. <u>2</u> **fantasies:** *imagined scenes*
4. <u>2</u> **ranch:** *farm, usually very large, for raising cattle, horses, or sheep, in the American West*
5. <u>3</u> **Westerns:** *books or movies which tell stories about the early days in the American West*

6. 3 **escape literature:** *fiction which people read to forget about their own lives*
7. 6 **astronaut:** *person trained to fly into space*
8. 12 **Midwest:** *central part of the United States, not including the most southern states*
9. 13 **Indians:** *a state in north central United States*
10. 14 **civilian:** *not a member of the Army, Navy, Marine Corps or Air Force*
11. 14 **test pilot:** *pilot who flies new kinds of planes to see how well they fly*
12. 16 **Apollo:** *(in Greek and Roman myths) the god of poetry, music, and medicine; spacecraft are sometimes named after characters from Greek and Roman myths*
13. 22 **flight mechanics:** *the study of how planes and spacecraft are able to fly*
14. 24 **weightlessness:** *having no weight*
15. 25 **gravity:** *weight due to the pull of the earth*
16. 26 **dive:** *act of moving quickly downward*
17. 28 **simulator:** *machine that gives the appearance of real conditions*
18. 29 **simulated:** *made to look like the real thing*
19. 30 **spacecraft:** *kind of plane which can go into outer space*
20. 33 **stranded:** *left with no way to return*
21. 37 **specific:** *particular*
22. 39 **geology:** *the study of the rocks and soil*
23. 43 **televised:** *shown on television*
24. 44 **Jr.:** *Junior; title for a son who has the same name as his father*
25. 45 **backpack:** *a pack for carrying things on your back, often made of canvas or nylon*
26. 51 **earthquakelike:** *resembling an earthquake*
27. 52 **reflector:** *something which sends light back in the direction it came from, like a mirror*
28. 56 **plaque:** *sign placed in public place on a statue, building, etc., often in memory of a special event*
29. 58 **concern:** *worry*
30. 59 **germs:** *very small living organisms that cannot be seen but cause disease*
31. 61 **scrubbed:** *washed thoroughly*
32. 62 **disinfectant:** *liquid that kills germs*

33. <u>65</u> **Ohio:** *a state in north central United States*
34. <u>66</u> **blurry:** *not clear*
35. <u>72</u> **shuttle:** *for transportation which goes between two points regularly*
36. <u>74</u> **frontier:** *boundary between the known and the unknown*

Skimming Exercise

1. According to the first paragraph, what games did American children play 50 years ago?

2. According to the second paragraph, what did Neil Armstrong study at Purdue University?

3. According to the fourth paragraph, what was the name of Armstrong's spacecraft?

4. According to the sixth paragraph, did the astronauts bring back any dangerous germs to earth?

Comprehension Questions

1. What kinds of games do American children play today and why?

2. What was Neil Armstrong's background before he joined the space program?

3. How did Armstrong prepare himself for the space program?

4. Why did the astronauts need to examine the landing surface of the moon before setting the rocket down?

5. Who went to the moon with Neil Armstrong on July 20, 1969?

6. What special equipment did they wear?

7. What did they do on the moon for science?

8. Where did Neil Armstrong go when he left the space program?

Cloze Exercise

Neil Armstrong was the first person to set 1_____ on the moon. He came from the 2_____ and studied to become an 3_____. He was also a 4_____ pilot for the Navy. To 5_____ himself for the space project he studied 6_____ subjects such as 7_____ theory and 8_____ mechanics. He also had to get used to the lack of 9_____ and learn how to 10_____ his spacecraft down on the 11_____. On July 20, 1969, he finally 12_____ on the moon. He 13_____ the surface, 14_____ rock samples, and 15_____ up scientific experiments.

Vocabulary Exercise

The affix *less* means "without." So *weightless* means "without weight" and *boundless* means "without bounds or limits." Add *less* to the following words and use them in a sentence.

1. time
2. change
3. window

4. air
5. use
6. harm

Discussion Questions

1. Do you believe exploring space is important for the future of mankind? Why or why not?

2. What kinds of knowledge can space exploration bring? What are the kinds of questions that it cannot answer?

3. Should every country have an individual space exploration program, only the larger ones, or should the exploration of space be programs of international cooperation, involving large and small countries together? Why?

4. Would you have liked to become an astronaut? Describe the reasons for your answer.

Writing Exercise

Describe what you believe is important about space exploration. If you think it is not important, what other major project would you want your country to study? Should such projects be paid for from private or public funds and why?

7 Ann Landers

Answer the following questions before you read the article.

1. If you were changed to a boy (girl), how would your life be different?
2. What are the advantages of being male? Disadvantages?
3. What are the advantages of being female? Disadvantages?
4. Give some examples of women's jobs.
5. Give some examples of men's jobs.
6. What is it important for a female to be or do?
7. What is it important for a male to be or do?

Dear Readers:

I read something recently that really blew me out of the water. In spite of all the back-breaking work of the women's movement and frontline heroines in the vanguard of business and industry, the prejudice 5 against females is still very strong.

In the February issue of *Redbook*, Dr. Alice Baumgartner and her colleagues at the Institute for Equality in Education at the University of Colorado surveyed 2,000 children throughout the state. They asked one question: "If you woke up tomorrow and discovered you were a 10 boy (or a girl), how would your life be different?"

The responses were startling. There was a serious lack of respect for females. In fact, they were held in contempt by both sexes. Many girls said if they were boys, their lives would be better economically and statuswise and they would enjoy more freedom and have a better 15 time with less responsibility. One girl said, "If I were a boy, my father might love me more."

Boys felt that if they were girls they would have to be beautiful and know how to put on makeup and dress well. "No one would be interested in my brain," said one respondent.

20 When boys considered the possibility that females could marry and work outside the home, the jobs they listed most often were secretaries, nurses, cocktail waitresses, social workers, models, airline stewardesses and prostitutes. "Boys still see women in roles as serving others," Dr. Baumgartner said.

25 The girls envisioned a variety of exciting career possibilities for themselves if they were boys. Most often mentioned were professional athletes, auto mechanics, construction workers, pilots, engineers, forest rangers, stuntmen, coal miners, sportscasters and farmers.

Many girls realized that one disadvantage of maleness is stoicism: 30 "If I were a boy, I would have to stay calm and cool whenever something happened. I would not be allowed to express my true feelings." Girls often felt that as boys they would have to be rowdy, macho and smart-alecky and show off more.

The bottom line seemed to be that boys knew they were valued 35 by their parents, but girls were not sure. They felt their brothers were the favorites.

Redbook asked, "What's a mother to do?" Their answers were thoughtful and constructive. (I've added some of my own.)

Start by finding out what your children think of the opposite sex.
40 If they have peculiar notions, set them straight—not in a critical manner
but an instructive one.

Don't divide chores by gender. Support your child's interests and
talents, whatever they are. Value your children equally and let them
know that you do.

45 Encourage your daughter's athletic interests as well as your son's.
Remember the power of example. Educate your sons and daughters
about stereotypes. Let them know boys and girls can do many of the
same things equally well. Have some spectacular examples that they
can relate to: physicians, lawyers, bankers, politicians, and don't forget
50 Supreme Court Justice Sandra Day O'Connor. (492 words)

Supreme Court Justice Sandra Day O'Connor

Vocabulary

1. <u>2</u> **blew me out of the water:** *shocked me*
2. <u>3</u> **back-breaking work:** *very hard work*
3. <u>3</u> **frontline:** *most advanced or responsible position*
4. <u>4</u> **vanguard:** *leading role*
5. <u>6</u> **Redbook:** *a women's magazine in the United States*
6. <u>7</u> **colleagues:** *people working in the same place, especially in a profession*
7. <u>11</u> **startling:** *shocking*

8. 12 **held in contempt:** *thought of as not valuable*
9. 14 **statuswise:** *in terms of status; with regard to social position*
10. 18 **makeup:** *powder, paint, etc., worn on the face*
11. 19 **respondent:** *person who answered the questions*
12. 23 **prostitutes:** *women or men who earn money by having sex with anyone who will pay for it*
13. 25 **envisioned:** *imagined*
14. 29 **stoicism:** *patience and courage when suffering*
15. 32 **rowdy:** *noisy and rough*
16. 33 **macho:** *aggressively masculine*
17. 33 **smart-alecky:** *claiming to know everything and trying to sound clever*
18. 33 **show off:** *behave so as to try to get admiration for oneself, one's abilities, etc.*
19. 34 **the bottom line seemed to be that:** *basically; the conclusion seemed to be that*
20. 38 **constructive:** *helpful*
21. 42 **chores:** *household work*
22. 42 **gender:** *classification by sex; male or female*
23. 47 **stereotypes:** *fixed patterns which are believed to represent types of people or events, but which do not take individual differences into account*
24. 48 **spectacular:** *striking; impressive*

Skimming Exercise

1. Did the children in the survey respect women?

2. What did the boys think would be important if they had to be girls?

3. How did the girls think they would have to act if they were boys?

True/False/Not enough information (?)

If a statement is false, rewrite it so that it is true.

T F ? 1. According to the author, the woman's movement has been successful and has brought women to a position equal to that of men.

T F ?   2. The children surveyed by Dr. Alice Baumgartner and her colleagues lived in Colorado.

T F ?   3. The children's responses were different from what the researchers expected.

T F ?   4. The girls who responded to the survey thought they wanted to be boys.

T F ?   5. The jobs that the boys considered wives could take were very limited.

T F ?   6. Girls were not interested in taking jobs that are generally considered to be men's jobs.

T F ?   7. The girls felt that girls are supposed to be calm and not express their feelings.

T F ?   8. The children felt that their parents tended to love sons more than daughters.

T F ?   9. Girls tend to be given work that is considered to be feminine.

T F ? 10. Women's athletic abilities are admired and valued.

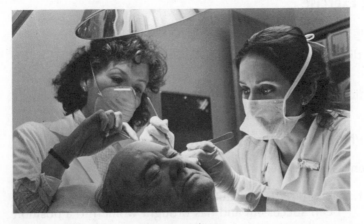

Dr. Jessica Fewkes examines a patient

Comprehension Questions

1. What is this reading about?
2. Were any adults surveyed?
3. Were females respected or looked down upon by the children who answered the question?
4. How did many girls think their lives would be better if they were boys?
5. What did the boys feel to be important for girls?
6. What careers did the girls envision for themselves if they were boys?
7. What characteristics did the girls think boys had?
8. How do children learn stereotypes?
9. What is a good way to show that boys and girls can do many of the same things equally well?
10. What careers are often thought of as masculine, but are equally open to women?

Cloze Exercise

The author was <u>1   </u> at the responses to the <u>2   </u> of two thousand <u>3   </u> by Dr. Alice Baumgartner and her <u>4   </u> , as reported in the February issue of *Redbook*. The <u>5   </u> to the survey were <u>6   </u>. The children were asked: "If you woke up <u>7   </u> and discovered you were a boy (or a girl), how would your <u>8   </u> be different?" Both boys and girls held females in <u>9   </u>. The girls felt that <u>10   </u> are valued more than <u>11   </u>. The boys considered only very limited career possibilities for <u>12   </u>.

Mothers seem to be partially responsible for the <u>13   </u>

that their children form, and they should try to demonstrate to

their __14_____ that both boys and girls can do __15_____

of the same things __16_____ well.

Vocabulary Exercises

A. Match the occupations on the left with the descriptions on the right.

1. _____ cocktail waitresses
2. _____ social workers
3. _____ models
4. _____ athletes
5. _____ auto mechanics
6. _____ construction workers
7. _____ forest rangers
8. _____ stuntmen
9. _____ coal miners
10. _____ sportscasters

a. workers in a coal mine, a deep hole or network of holes under the ground, from which coal is dug
b. they build buildings
c. people who engage in radio or TV broadcasts of sporting news or sporting events
d. people who compete in sports that call for special physical abilities
e. women who serve drinks in bars and restaurants
f. people trained to help others with problems of health, housing, etc.
g. people in charge of tree-covered lands
h. they repair automobiles
i. people who wear clothes or use products to display to possible buyers in a shop, or to be photographed, etc.
j. men who do dangerous things in a film so that the actors do not have to take risks

B.   Change these verbs to nouns ending in -*ment* or some form of
     -*ion*.

     1. educate   4. express
     2. excite   5. divide
     3. enjoy   6. relate

Discussion Questions

1. Compare your answers to the seven questions placed before the
    article itself with your partner's answers to the same questions.

2. How do the attitudes of the respondents in the survey toward
    women compare to those of people in your culture?

3. Do you think your attitudes toward women are typical in your
    culture? If not, how are your attitudes different?

4. Are you satisfied with being a female/male? Why or why not?

Writing Exercise

Describe the way you think a girl should be brought up, and what
kind of a future is the best for a girl. Then describe the way a boy
should be brought up. If there are differences, explain why.

   If you were brought up in another way, describe that, and whether
there were any problems in the way you were brought up.

8
The Birdwoman of Falmouth

Falmouth, Cape Cod—A charming woman . . . A house filled with miscellaneous objects . . . including three wild starlings . . . that can talk!

What? The birds live *with* the woman? *Inside* the house? They
5 *talk?*

Yet it's all true. Talking wild starlings share the home of 56-year-old Margarete Sigl Corbo, companion of birds.

On the day of my visit, Margarete, a cheerful, square-faced woman,

Margarete Corbo and Pele

freed three specimens of *European starling* from their aviary by the
10 television. They perched on the couch, the curtain rod, the backs of
chairs. It was noon, time for the starlings, Mikey, Pele, and Mortimer,
to bathe, Corbo said.

One at a time, the birds came fluttering down to the floor to
vibrate their wings and duck their heads in an orange plastic tub. In
15 a minute, feathers rustled and fluttered as the starlings flew about
drying themselves. Then they landed gently on shoulders, heads,
sweaters, and shoes, poking and pecking and prying under books,
into hair.

Pele made conversation: "Mortimer, give me a kiss," he said.
20 "Sing me a song; sing me a song."

"They like company," said Margarete Corbo as Pele climbed down
from her hair to her shoulder. When Corbo said, "Kissee, kissee," the
starling reached up and touched its beak to her lips.

"They're always busy. They love helping me vacuum or clean the
25 dishes. What clowns they are! Of all the pets I've had, they're honestly
the friendliest to bring up."

After half an hour, she returned the birds to their cage where
they continued to talk. That is, Pele talked, while the others whistled
and called "whooee."

30 To most people the starling is an annoyance. "Most quarrelsome
and aggressive," says one book. "A major pest," says another. And
another says, "a naturalized American citizen of questionable char-
acter." This refers to the fact that, like most Americans, including
Corbo, starlings came here as immigrants. They were brought here in
35 the late 1800's by a New York drug manufacturer. He decided to
introduce into America every species of bird which Shakespeare
mentioned in his plays. Eighty pairs of starlings arrived in New York
City and quickly multiplied. There are now millions spread across the
entire United States. People who love to feed birds complain that the
40 starlings crowd out all the other birds and eat the birdseed themselves.
Others complain that the great flocks of birds are too noisy and dirty.

Corbo thinks they are unpopular because of prejudice. "It's
discrimination," she exclaims. "I immigrated, too; I feel just like the
starlings. Although they've done well in this country, Americans resent
45 their progress. Even so, the starlings manage to take care of themselves
very well."

Maybe if the starlings want to fight their bad publicity, they'll all
have to learn how to talk! (461 words)

Vocabulary

1. <u>T</u> **birdwoman:** *woman, so called by other people because she loves and lives with birds*
2. <u>T</u> **Falmouth:** *a town in southeastern Massachusetts*
3. <u>1</u> **Cape Cod:** *long, curving peninsula in southeastern Massachusetts*
4. <u>2</u> **miscellaneous:** *many different kinds of*
5. <u>2</u> **starlings:** *dark-colored birds, originally European, and now widespread in North America*
6. <u>9</u> **aviary:** *cage or other similar place where birds are kept*
7. <u>10</u> **couch:** *piece of furniture, often with a back, for sitting or lying on; sofa*
8. <u>13</u> **fluttering:** *moving their wings lightly and rapidly*
9. <u>14</u> **duck:** *lower briefly (into water)*
10. <u>14</u> **plastic:** *strong, light, man-made chemical material which can be manufactured in many shapes for many different uses*
11. <u>15</u> **rustled:** *moved with soft, light sounds*
12. <u>17</u> **poking:** *pushing, with short, quick movements*
13. <u>17</u> **prying:** *searching by pushing between or under objects*

14. <u>22</u> **kissee:** *(baby talk) "Give me a kiss."*
15. <u>23</u> **beak:** *hard, pointed part of a bird's mouth*
16. <u>24</u> **vacuum:** *clean a room using a vacuum cleaner*
17. <u>25</u> **clowns:** *persons who entertain by jokes, tricks, etc., often in a circus*
18. <u>26</u> **bring up:** *raise; take care of*
19. <u>29</u> **whooee:** *word with no special meaning, probably used to call attention or express joy*
20. <u>30</u> **annoyance:** *disturbance; irritation*
21. <u>30</u> **quarrelsome:** *often quarreling; fighting (with other birds)*
22. <u>31</u> **aggressive:** *often attacking (other birds) and invading (other birds') territory*
23. <u>31</u> **pest:** *annoying, harmful plant or animal*
24. <u>32</u> **naturalized:** *of foreign birth but having (American) citizenship*
25. <u>32</u> **questionable:** *doubtful, uncertain, possibly bad*
26. <u>40</u> **birdseed:** *mixture of various kinds of seeds used for feeding birds*
27. <u>43</u> **discrimination:** *bad treatment of people of a different race or cultural tradition*
28. <u>43</u> **immigrated:** *came from a foreign country to live*
29. <u>45</u> **even so:** *however; in spite of that*
30. <u>47</u> **publicity:** *information (about starlings); reputation*

True/False/Not enough information (?)

If a statement is false, rewrite it so that it is true.

T F ? 1. Three starlings share a home with Margarete and a companion of birds.

T F ? 2. The starlings took a bath in an orange plastic tub.

T F ? 3. Pele asked Margarete for a kiss.

T F ? 4. Pele touched its lips to Margarete's beak.

T F ? 5. Margarete has had other pets besides her starlings.

T F ?   6. All three of the birds can talk.

T F ?   7. Starlings are major pets, according to a book.

T F ?   8. Both Ms. Corbo and starlings are immigrants to America.

T F ?   9. Ms. Corbo was brought to America in the late 1800's.

T F ? 10. Ms. Corbo sympathizes with starlings because she im-
              migrated to America, too.

Comprehension Questions

1. The writer's purpose, in the first paragraph, is _____.

    a. to tell about three talking starlings
    b. to tell about a charming woman
    c. to tell what the story is about and interest the reader in the
        subject
    d. to tell about the Birdwoman of Falmouth

2. The second paragraph (line 4) expresses the writer's _____.

    a. surprise
    b. anger
    c. joy
    d. dislike

3. Paragraphs four through nine (lines 8–29) tell mainly about

    _____.

    a. what the birds did and said
    b. what Ms. Corbo did and said
    c. Ms. Corbo's conversation with the birds
    d. the writer's visit to Ms. Corbo's house

4. The fifth paragraph (from line 13) tells us mainly about

    _____.

    a. the birds taking a bath
    b. the birds' plastic bathtub
    c. the birds fluttering down to the floor
    d. the birds' noon meal

5. The tenth, eleventh, and twelfth paragraphs (lines 30–48) tell us mainly _____.

    a. the history of starlings in America, the opinions of Ms. Corbo, and the writer's comments

    b. why people don't like starlings

    c. why people don't like immigrants

    d. why Ms. Corbo likes starlings

Vocabulary Exercises

A. Find three words for each of these word roots. Use the article and your dictionary.

    1. -quest-
    2. -turn-
    3. -natur-
    4. -clud-
    5. -tele-
    6. -migrat-

B. Margarete Corbo's birds whistle. Can you match the sounds below to the name of the animal that makes that sound?

    1. lion   _____ hiss

    2. cat   _____ neigh

    3. dog   _____ roar

    4. frog   _____ buzz

    5. bee   _____ croak

    6. snake   _____ moo

    7. cow   _____ bark

    8. horse   _____ purr

Which of the animals above could make this kind of motion?

_____ crouch   _____ trot

_____ fly   _____ gallop

_____ slither   _____ hop

Discussion Questions

1. Do you think you could train a bird or an animal? Have you ever tried? If you did, how did you do it? If you haven't, how do you think you could do it?

2. Why do people like to have animals and birds as pets? What is the difference between people interacting with each other and people interacting with pets?

Writing Exercise

Pretend that you have just visited Margarete Corbo. Write a letter to a friend describing the woman and her pets. You can add your own opinions of her way of life.

III. Native Americans

Pueblo women making pottery

9 Hopi Indian Doctor

A snowstorm was coming; the wind was blowing hard across the Hopi Reservation in Arizona. In the late afternoon, John Begay, a Navaho man, parked his pickup truck at Tochi's door. He wanted Tochi to go with him to see his sick wife, who was 150 miles away in their home
5 at the foot of the mountains.

Tochi is a Hopi doctor. If I were to call him a medicine man, many Americans would think he used magic in treating his patients. He doesn't use witchcraft, but he does listen to the patient's thoughts as well as look after the patient's body.

10   Tochi asked Begay many questions about his wife. How old was she? How long had she been ill? Where was the pain? Then Tochi chose medicines from his collection. Each medicine had been made from a desert plant. He had to take quite a lot of each medicine since he would be too far away to get more.

15   Tochi and Begay drove through the night; the snow had stopped falling when they reached the Navaho home. The Hopi Indian Reservation is on high land in the middle of the Navaho Indian Reservation. The Hopi doctor had traveled half-way across the reservation to reach his patient.

20   Tochi prepared tea from brown dry leaves and helped the woman to drink it. "You'll feel better after you drink this," he assured her, and smiled when she made a face at the bitter taste. He knew that if the medicine tasted like water, it would not seem powerful. This medicine was always good for fever. But Tochi could see that his

25   patient was a very sick woman. He planned his treatment carefully. He had to take one step at a time. If the medicine did not work, the reason must be that it was either not the right one or not strong enough. Tochi would keep changing medicines until he found the right one. Meanwhile, he would keep the patient cheerful and confi-

30   dent. That was necessary for a cure.

For four days the Hopi doctor sat by the sick woman. Then he saw that his patient was better. By nighttime he knew that his work was done. He said he would be ready to start for home in the morning.

If this woman had been taken to a hospital, she might have insisted

35   on having an Indian doctor come to see her. Many Indians live in very lonely places on the reservations and do not trust non-Indian ways. Some physicians understand this, and let the patients have their medicine men as well as their western-style doctors.

During the night another snowstorm began. When Tochi and

40   Begay started out, going south from Navaho Mountain, the storm did not give them trouble. The snow fell, but the strong winds blew it away. But as they crossed the open desert, the snow became worse and worse. Finally, the truck got stuck in the snow. It was getting dark, and they were too far from any village to try walking through

45   the deep snow. Tochi and Begay stayed in the truck all night. They wrapped themselves in a blanket and stamped their feet to keep them warm. The next day, they walked back and forth to keep warm as the snow kept falling. They slept in the truck again that night. "I think they will come to find us tomorrow," Tochi said.

50   After another day of waiting, Tochi made up his mind to find his
way to help. He started out on foot, and after half an hour he came
upon the tracks of some sheep. He followed the tracks, hoping they
would lead him to people. The trail continued for two miles, straight
to a Navaho home, with smoke rising from the chimney. Without
55 asking any questions, the Navahos offered Tochi coffee and hot food.
Then Tochi and the two Navahos set out on horses and rescued the
truck and its driver.

A Hopi doctor's house call totaled eight days, including two days
without food in a desert snowstorm! (677 words)

Vocabulary

1. <u>T</u>   **Hopi:** *a group of North American Indians who live in the
    northeastern part of Arizona*
2. <u>1</u>   **snowstorm:** *storm with heavy snowfall and high winds*
3. <u>2</u>   **reservation:** *land set aside by the United States government
    which belongs to a particular group of American Indians*
4. <u>2</u>   **Arizona:** *a state in the southwestern part of the United
    States*
5. <u>2</u>   **Navaho:** *a group of North American Indians living in the
    northeastern part of Arizona*
6. <u>3</u>   **pickup truck:** *light truck with an open body and low sides*
7. <u>8</u>   **witchcraft:** *the practice of magic*
8. <u>22</u> **made a face:** *put an expression of dislike on (her) face*
9. <u>36</u> **non-Indian ways:** *customs of people who are not Indians*
10. <u>43</u> **got stuck:** *became unable to move*
11. <u>58</u> **house call:** *visit by a doctor to a patient's house*

True/False/Not enough information (?)

If a statement is false, rewrite it so that it is true.

T F ?   1. John Begay is a Navaho.

T F ?   2. John Begay's wife is sick.

T F ?   3. Tochi uses witchcraft in treating his patients.

T F ?   4. Tochi asked Begay's wife many questions.

T F ?   5. Tochi and Begay drove all night to reach Begay's house.

T F ?   6. Tochi knew that if the medicine tasted bitter, it would seem powerful.

T F ?   7. Tochi is a western-style doctor.

T F ?   8. There is a hospital on the Hopi Reservation.

T F ?   9. The snow became worse and worse as Tochi and Begay went across the desert.

T F ? 10. Tochi walked from where the truck was stuck to a Navaho home.

Hopi village

Comprehension Questions

1. Why did John Begay come to see Tochi?
2. In what way does Tochi treat his patients?
3. Why did Tochi have to take a lot of each medicine?

4. Is the Hopi Indian Reservation inside or outside of the Navaho Indian Reservation?

5. Besides medicine, what was necessary for curing Begay's wife?

6. How did the Hopi doctor know that his work was done on the evening of the fourth day?

7. Why do some physicians let Indian patients have their medicine men as well as western-style doctors?

8. Why did Tochi and Begay stay in the truck all night?

9. How many nights did Tochi and Begay sleep in the truck?

10. How did Tochi find the Navaho home?

Sequence Exercise

Complete the sentences with one of the following words: *first, before, when, after, while, then, finally, during.*

1. _____ parking his pickup truck, John Begay asked Tochi to go with him to see his sick wife.

2. _____ Tochi asked Begay many questions about his wife.

3. _____ Tochi chose medicines from his collection.

4. The snow had stopped falling _____ they reached Begay's home.

5. _____ Begay's wife made a face at the bitter taste of the medicine, Tochi smiled.

6. Tochi kept his patient cheerful and confident _____ trying different medicines.

7. _____ four days, he saw that his patient was better.

8. _____ Tochi and Begay started out from Begay's home, the storm did not give them trouble.

9. As they crossed the desert, the storm became worse and worse, and _____ the truck got stuck in the snow.

10. _____ the next two nights, Tochi and Begay stayed in the truck.

11. _____, Tochi walked to a Navaho home to get help.

Discussion Questions

1. Compare medical treatment in your culture as it is today with the way it was for your parents and grandparents.

2. Do you believe that it is important to trust your doctor and to believe that you will get well? How does that influence your illness?

Writing Exercise

Pretend you are the Hopi doctor. Write to a friend describing your visit to the sick woman, your treatment of her, and what happened to you on the way back.

10
Alaskan Arts and Crafts

Art and beauty have always been part of everyday life in the Alaskan native culture. Household objects, tools, and decorative objects are both useful and beautiful. Materials that are easily available, such as animal skins, bone, ivory, wood, and grass, are transformed into works
5 of art that have now found a market. The native craftspeople made these objects for the same purposes as they are made all over the world. Wonderful masks were made for dances; baskets were made for many uses; bits of stone and ivory were carved into animals and people during the long Alaskan winter nights.

10 European and American influences are seen in some of the crafts. Scrimshaw, drawing on ivory, was originally done by New England sailors on whaling ships during the months at sea. Now it is a favorite art form of Alaskan craftspeople. Printmaking was introduced only recently, but fine artists are now turning out unique prints. The
15 subjects of the sculpture and prints reflect stories and myths which the Alaskan culture has preserved.

In the shops you can find carvings in jade, ivory, and stone; prints, paintings, and pottery; clothing and jewelry; baskets and toys. If you're looking for authentic Alaskan arts and crafts you should watch for the
20 symbols which tell you "made in Alaska." The "Silver Hand" symbol means that the article was made by an Alaskan Eskimo, Aleut, or Indian craftsperson or artist. The "Alaskan Resident" symbol means that it was made in Alaska by a resident artist or craftsperson. Without either of these symbols, the article may have been made "outside", either
25 elsewhere in the United States or somewhere abroad. These two craft symbols mean authentic value for the higher prices charged.

"Silver Hand"

"Alaska Resident"

Materials Used by Alaskan Craftspeople

Grass, Roots, Bark

Alaskan Eskimo and Indian baskets are made from many native
30 materials: beach grass, often interwoven with seal gut; marsh grass;
tree roots; cedar and birchbark; whalebone from the mouth of the
bowhead whale. Athabaskan Indian women pick birch bark for baskets
in June when it has a honey-gold color. Spruce and willow roots are
split and used to sew the baskets.

Basketry, carving and weaving

35 Gold nuggets

Only a small fraction of the gold mined in the world is like the natural
nuggets found in streams in Alaska. Because they are so rare, the price
of natural nuggets on the open market is higher than the price of
gold. The price goes up according to the size of the nugget. Alaskan
40 gold nuggets are made into beautiful jewelry, such as pendants,
watchbands, earrings, rings, and other items.

Jade

Jade, Alaska's state gem, must be cut with diamond and carborundum tools because it is so hard. Jade from Canada and Alaska is often sent
45 to Europe and the Far East for cutting and then it comes back to Alaska. Much of the jade used by Alaskan craftspeople comes from quarries near Kotzebue in northwestern Alaska. It is turned into jewelry, sculpture, bookends, clocks, and lamp bases.

Ivory

50 Only Alaskan Natives are allowed to hunt, harvest, and possess unworked ivory, and it cannot be sold until it is handcrafted. Walrus ivory is found in three forms. Fresh new ivory is gleaming white. Old ivory is found on beaches and is usually tan or brown. Fossilized ivory can come from the tusks of both walrus and the long-extinct mastodon
55 and is usually dark brown, sometimes with bluish overtones; this is the rarest variety. The ivory is used in scrimshaw work, jewelry, and figurines.

Unlike many other marine mammals, the walrus is in no danger of extinction. Walruses are hunted for both their meat and tusks by
60 the Eskimos of the Arctic Ocean and Bering Sea regions. These homely animals are actually more plentiful now than they were in the 1800's, when they were first hunted commercially.

Soapstone

Softer than ivory or jade, soapstone is easily worked into a wide variety
65 of exquisite sculptures. Animals are particularly popular subjects. The smooth lustrous surface of a finished piece feels slightly soapy to the touch, and must be waxed or oiled to preserve its unique texture and appearance. Although many kinds of soapstone are found in Alaska, most of the stone used in these carvings is quarried in the Pacific
70 Northwest and Canada. Soapstone varies in color from the common dark green to brown, dark orange, light gray, and tan.

Bowl with fish and bird symbols

Wood

In the Bering Sea and Arctic Ocean areas where there are no trees, driftwood is used to make masks and other craft items. In interior
75 Alaska, birch and birchbark are used to make traditional household utensils. Southeastern Alaska has yellow cedar, which is used to carve masks, intricately cut boxes, and totems. The use of wood in arts and handicrafts is widespread and you'll find many such items throughout the state. (798 words)

Vocabulary

1. <u>T</u>   **Alaskan:** *of Alaska, one of the Unites States, west of Canada, separated from mainland United States*
2. <u>2</u>   **decorative:** *used for decoration; attractive*
3. <u>5</u>   **craftspeople:** *highly skilled workers*
4. <u>11</u>   **New England:** *from the region made up of the states of Maine, New Hampshire, Vermont, Massachusetts, Connecticut, and Rhode Island*
5. <u>12</u>   **whaling:** *the hunting of whales*
6. <u>13</u>   **printmaking:** *making of pictures engraved or carved on sheets of metal, wood or other materials, then covered with ink and pressed onto paper*
7. <u>17</u>   **jade:** *a semi-precious stone, usually green*
8. <u>19</u>   **authentic:** *real; genuine*

 9. <u>21</u> **Eskimo:** *race of people living in northern Alaska*
10. <u>21</u> **Aleut:** *race of people living on the Aleutian Islands*
11. <u>27</u> **bark:** *heavy outer cover of a tree's trunk and branches*
12. <u>30</u> **interwoven:** *woven together*
13. <u>30</u> **seal:** *an animal with fur that lives in the sea*
14. <u>30</u> **gut:** *a strong thread made from an animal's intestines*
15. <u>31</u> **cedar:** *a tall evergreen tree with hard, reddish, sweet-smelling wood*
16. <u>31</u> **birch:** *any of several trees, common in northern countries, with paper-like, easily peeled bark*
17. <u>31</u> **whalebone:** *bone from a whale*
18. <u>32</u> **bowhead whale:** *type of whale*
19. <u>32</u> **Athabaskan:** *a tribe of Alaskan Indians*
20. <u>33</u> **spruce:** *an evergreen tree with short, pointed needles and soft wood*
21. <u>35</u> **nuggets:** *small pieces or lumps of a precious metal found in the earth*
22. <u>40</u> **pendants:** *necklaces*
23. <u>41</u> **watchbands:** *bands made of leather, cloth, metal, etc., by which watches are kept fastened to wrists*
24. <u>43</u> **carborundum:** *a very hard substance*
25. <u>46</u> **quarries:** *places from which stone is dug*
26. <u>48</u> **bookends:** *supports at each end of a row of books*
27. <u>51</u> **walrus:** *an animal with long tusks that lives in the sea*
28. <u>53</u> **tan:** *yellowish brown*
29. <u>53</u> **fossilized:** *turned into stone over hundreds of thousands of years*
30. <u>54</u> **tusks:** *very long pointed teeth which come out beyond the mouth*
31. <u>54</u> **long-extinct:** *did exist but died out a long time ago*
32. <u>54</u> **mastodon:** *very large animal that looked something like an elephant with long fur*
33. <u>55</u> **overtones:** *colors that you see only traces of when looking at another color*
34. <u>57</u> **figurines:** *small ornamental animal or human figures made of baked clay, cut stone, etc.*
35. <u>58</u> **marine:** *living in the sea*
36. <u>58</u> **mammals:** *a group of animals whose females give milk to feed their young*

37. <u>60</u> **Bering Sea:** *sea between Alaska and the USSR*
38. <u>60</u> **homely:** *not good looking*
39. <u>62</u> **commercially:** *for profit*
40. <u>66</u> **lustrous:** *shining*
41. <u>67</u> **texture:** *degree of roughness or smoothness*
42. <u>70</u> **Pacific Northwest:** *northwestern states of the U.S., along the Pacific Coast*
43. <u>74</u> **driftwood:** *wood that has been washed up on shore*
44. <u>76</u> **utensils:** *tools*
45. <u>77</u> **intricately:** *having many elements arranged in a complex way*
46. <u>77</u> **totems:** *images of animals, plants, or natural objects, often carved on a pole, serving among certain primitive peoples as the emblem of a clan or family*

Skimming Exercise

1. What materials do Alaskan natives use for their arts and crafts?
2. What are the two symbols used to identify Alaskan arts and crafts?
3. What is Alaska's state gem?
4. How many kinds of ivory are there?
5. What is the most common color of soapstone?
6. Where is driftwood used for crafts?

True/False/Not enough information (?)

If a statement is false, rewrite it so that it is true.

T F ?   1. Alaskan artists use tin and plastic in their products.

T F ?   2. New England sailors on whaling ships made scrimshaw objects.

T F ?   3. The "Silver Hand" emblem tells you that an item was made outside Alaska.

T   F   ?   4.   The "Alaskan Resident" emblem tells you that an item was made by an Eskimo.

T   F   ?   5.   All of the items sold in Alaska are made in Alaska.

T   F   ?   6.   The emblems on Alaskan arts and crafts tell you exactly how much an item costs.

T   F   ?   7.   Alaskan baskets are made from many different types of grasses.

T   F   ?   8.   Cotton and silk thread are used by Indian women to sew their baskets together.

T   F   ?   9.   Gold nuggets are worthless because they are easy to find.

T   F   ?   10.   Jade is always carved at the same place it is quarried.

T   F   ?   11.   Mastodons are now extinct.

T   F   ?   12.   Walruses are now extinct.

T   F   ?   13.   Soapstone is used for bathing.

T   F   ?   14.   Trees are very common all over Alaska.

T   F   ?   15.   Oak and pine trees grow in Alaska's interior.

Comprehension Questions

1.   What has influenced the subjects of prints and sculptures?

2.   What kinds of items can be found in Alaskan gift shops?

3.   Why should you look for the "Silver Hand" and "Alaskan Resident" symbols?

4.   When is birchbark for baskets picked?

5. Why is the cost of gold nuggets higher on the open market than the cost of other forms of gold?

6. What kinds of tools are used to cut jade?

7. Who is allowed to hunt and harvest ivory?

8. Where does fossilized ivory come from?

9. Why must soapstone carvings be waxed or oiled?

10. Where does soapstone come from?

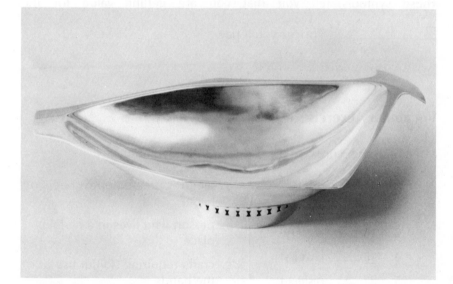

Silver bowl, ca. 1977, by Ron Seningetuk

Cloze Exercise

Alaska's native peoples have created tools both <u>1   </u>
and beautiful, and decorative items <u>2   </u> from
many materials. Some crafts have been influenced by crafts from
<u>3   </u> and <u>4   </u>. The subjects of prints
and sculptures are influenced by Alaskan stories and <u>5   </u>.

The "6_____ 7_____" symbol   means

that the item on which it appears was   8_____   by an

Alaskan Eskimo, Aleut, or Indian craftsperson or   9_____.

The "Resident Alaskan" emblem   10_____   that the article

was made in Alaska by a   11_____   artist or craftsperson.

These   symbols   tell   you   that   you   are   getting   value   for   the

12_____   prices you'll pay.

Vocabulary Exercise

A.   Match the words on the left with their definitions.

1.   14 _____ **prints**
2.   17 _____ **carvings**
3.   18 _____ **pottery**
4.   18 _____ **jewelry**
5.   22 _____ **resident**
6.   41 _____ **earrings**
7.   48 _____ **bookends**
8.   66 _____ **soapy**
9.   78 _____ **handicrafts**
10.   78 _____ **widespread**

a. pictures pressed onto sheets of paper

b. person who lives in a certain place

c. crafts requiring skillful use of the hands

d. things made of baked clay

e. supports at the ends of a row of books

f. things made by carving

g. rings, necklaces, and so on

h. ornaments worn on the ears

i. found in many places

j. like soap

B. Fill in the blanks.

1. _____

   a. This museum has many fine _____ings.

   b. The artist _____ed a portrait of an Eskimo.

   c. What color _____ do you want on this wall?

2. _____

   a. We went swimming at the old rock _____.

   b. Jade is _____ed in Alaska and Canada.

   c. Granite stone is cut at many _____ies in the Mid-west.

3. _____

   a. Authentic Alaskan artifacts are hand _____ed.

   b. A good _____sperson isn't easy to find these days.

   c. Writing is both an art and a _____.

4. _____

   a. This _____ing is made from jade.

   b. Who will _____ the Thanksgiving turkey?

   c. My father _____ed these statues out of wood from trees in his own yard.

5. _____

   a. Don't let prejudice _____ your decision.

   b. Western traders had a great _____ on Alaskan arts.

   c. The mayor is a very _____tial man in this town.

11 American Indians

Thousands of years ago a narrow land bridge connected Asia and North America. The people who were to become American Indians crossed that bridge from Asia 12,000 to 25,000 years ago. They gradually spread through Alaska into the rest of North America and eventually
5 into South America.

"The Buffalo Hunt" by Ma-Pe-Wi, Zia Pueblo, NM

Many different Indian cultures developed. In what is now Latin America, the Incas, Mayas, and Aztecs created great civilizations with large cities. The Plains Indians of North America did not build cities; they were nomadic tribes who lived in tents and followed the huge
10 buffalo herds. There are ancient ruins left by other North American Indians who built structures like apartment buildings against the cliff walls; Pueblo Indians still live in this kind of structure. These settled Indians lived by cultivating crops and developed important vegetables like corn and potatoes.

15   At first the Indians and the European settlers had friendly relations in what would later become the United States. Indians helped the Europeans learn to adapt to their hostile new environment, teaching them to hunt, fish, and grow crops. Some of the early settlements might not have survived if it had not been for help from friendly
20 Indians.

However, the settlers' desire for more and more land soon brought the Indians and the settlers into conflict. The Indians had no concept of private ownership of the land where their ancestors had lived for generations. Many of the white settlers thought that the Indians were
25 no more than ignorant savages who had no claim to the land.

In 1834 the United States government tried to solve the problem by giving the Indians all the land west of the Mississippi River, land considered undesirable by white settlers. Money was allocated by Congress to compensate Indians for their land and for having to move
30 west, but much of that money ended up in the pockets of federal officials. The journey west was long and hard, and many Indians died on the way. The land they moved to was promised to the Indians for "as long as the grass grows and the water runs." Only fourteen years later, however, gold was discovered in California, and access to the
35 gold fields was looked for. At the same time, there were increasing demands to open more land for settlement. As settlers and miners moved onto or through Indian land, Indians were forced onto increasingly smaller and less desirable pieces of land. This was typical of Europeans' and white Americans' dealings with Indians. One Indian
40 said that the white men had made many promises, more than he could remember, but they had only kept one. They promised to take the Indians' land, and they took it.

In defending their land, Indians gained a reputation for savagery. While this is not entirely unjustified, it must be remembered that it is
45 the winners of wars who usually write the history books. For example, many history books mention the killing of white women and children by Indians, but few mention the killing of Indian women and children by white soldiers.

Though many of the Indian leaders were brilliant military strate-
50 gists, their efforts to defend their lands ended in failure. Most of the fighting was with bows and arrows against guns, and the Indians were divided into many tribal groups while the whites were united against them.

By 1890, fighting between the government and the Indians had
55 ended. Most Indians lived on reservations, which they were not
allowed to leave without permission. Many of their religious and social
customs were banned. The aim of government policies was to try to
assimilate Indians into the white culture and decrease Indian land
holdings. It was not until the 1920's that these policies began to change.

Monument Valley, AZ

60   Most Indians still live on reservations even though they are now
free to live anywhere they like. Life on the reservation does not equip
Indians to survive in the larger culture. Many Indian values are
diametrically opposed to the values of the American mainstream
culture. Indians find private ownership of land hard to accept, and
65 they believe that the land and its produce belong to all members of a
group. They tend not to be materialistic or competitive, sharing what
little they have with others and preferring to assist others rather than
to compete with them.
Indians are, as a group, far below the national average in education,
70 income, and health. More than half of them have less than an eighth

grade education. Unemployment on some reservations runs as high as 75%, and 80% of all Indians who live on reservations have incomes below the poverty level. A combination of infectious diseases, malnutrition, and suicide makes the life expectancy of Indians about six
75 years below the national average.

In the 1960's, an Indian activist movement developed, drawing attention to Indians and their problems. Since then the government has become somewhat more responsive to Indian problems and less paternalistic. Indian leaders have been able to become more involved
80 in decisions about education, medical care, and so on. Indians have a new pride in their culture and history, and non-Indian Americans are beginning to have an appreciation of the values of Indian culture.
(865 words)

Vocabulary

1. <u>7</u>   **Latin America:** *all of the Western Hemisphere south of the United States*
2. <u>8</u>   **Plains Indians:** *Indians who lived on the Great Plains, the vast, flat area in the central part of the United States*
3. <u>9</u>   **nomadic:** *without a fixed home; wandering about, usually in search of food*
4. <u>9</u>   **tribes:** *groups of people or families living together under a leader*
5. <u>10</u>   **buffalo:** *a type of wild ox with a big head, and shoulders covered with long hair*
6. <u>15</u>   **settlers:** *people who go to live in an area where there have been few people before*
7. <u>22</u>   **concept:** *general idea, thought, or understanding*
8. <u>23</u>   **ownership:** *the state of owning something*
9. <u>27</u>   **Mississippi River:** *the longest river in the United States, running from Minnesota to the Gulf of Mexico*
10. <u>28</u>   **allocated:** *set aside for a special purpose*
11. <u>29</u>   **compensate:** *give payment of some kind to someone who has suffered a loss*
12. <u>30</u>   **ended up:** *reached a particular place or situation*
13. <u>30</u>   **federal:** *of the central government*
14. <u>34</u>   **access:** *path over which one has the right to pass*

15. <u>35</u>   **gold fields:** *land where gold was found*
16. <u>36</u>   **miners:** *people whose work is taking minerals out of the earth*
17. <u>43</u>   **savagery:** *the quality of being cruel or violent*
18. <u>49</u>   **strategists:** *people skilled in planning, especially military movements*
19. <u>55</u>   **Indian reservations:** *pieces of land set aside by the United States government for Indians to live on*
20. <u>57</u>   **banned:** *forbidden, especially by law*
21. <u>58</u>   **assimilate:** *absorb members of one social group into another social group*
22. <u>59</u>   **holdings:** *land in one's possession*
23. <u>63</u>   **diametrically:** *completely; totally*
24. <u>63</u>   **mainstream:** *of the main way of thinking or living in a certain place or country*
25. <u>66</u>   **materialistic:** *believing that material things are more important than spiritual values*
26. <u>71</u>   **runs as high as:** *becomes as high as*
27. <u>73</u>   **poverty level:** *the minimum amount of income, established by the government, which a family needs to live on*
28. <u>73</u>   **infectious:** *able to be spread from one person to another*
29. <u>73</u>   **malnutrition:** *an unhealthy condition of the body due to not getting enough food, or not enough of the right kind of food*
30. <u>74</u>   **life expectancy:** *average age to which one can be expected to live*
31. <u>76</u>   **activist movement:** *political movement for change*
32. <u>78</u>   **responsive:** *reacting quickly or in an understanding way*
33. <u>79</u>   **paternalistic:** *protecting people without allowing them freedom, treating them as if they were children*
34. <u>81</u>   **non-Indian Americans:** *Americans who are not Indians*

Skimming Exercise

Tell what happened in each of the following years or decades.

1. 1834

2. 1890

3. 1960's

True/False/Not enough information (?)

If a statement is false, rewrite it so that it is true.

T F ? 　1.　Indians came to North America from Asia by way of Alaska 12,000 to 25,000 years ago.

T F ? 　2.　Although they were spread out over a huge area, most Indian cultures were similar to one another.

T F ? 　3.　Plains Indians moved around, following buffalo herds.

T F ? 　4.　From the beginning, Indians fought with European settlers.

T F ? 　5.　Indians who owned land wouldn't sell it to white settlers, and this caused conflicts between Indians and settlers.

T F ? 　6.　When gold was discovered in California, miners needed to cross the land where the Indians lived to get to the gold fields.

T F ? 　7.　Whites often promised land to Indians but if the whites found a use for the land they took it back.

T F ? 　8.　In the late 1800's and early 1900's the United States government tried to make Indians become part of the general white population.

T F ? 　9.　Indians who leave the reservation usually do well, because Indian values help them succeed in the larger culture.

T F ? 10.　As a group, Indians are very poor.

Comprehension Questions

1.　When and by what route did the first Indians come to the Americas?

2. What two North American Indian groups does the writer describe, and how were they different?

3. How did Indians help the early settlers?

4. Why did some white settlers think that Indians didn't have any right to the land they lived on?

5. In 1834 did white settlers want the land west of the Mississippi?

6. Did many Indians get paid for their land and for having to move when the United States government moved them west of the Mississippi? If not, what happened to the money from Congress?

7. What year was gold discovered in California?

8. What happened to the Indians after that?

9. What is one reason that the Indians have a reputation for being savages?

10. What one thing did the Indians have in their favor in the fight for their land? What two things worked against them?

11. In what ways were Indians on reservations restricted in the late 1800's and early 1900's?

12. Why do Indians often have difficulty adjusting to the larger American culture?

13. How do Indians compare with other Americans in health, education, and income?

14. How has the Indian activist movement changed the attitude of the United States government? The roles of Indian leaders? The attitudes of other Americans?

Outline Exercise

I. Early History

  A. People who were to be later called Indians

    1. came to the Americas <u>1   </u>-25,000 years ago

    2. came from <u>2   </u> by way of land <u>3   </u>

  B. Indian Cultures

    1. many <u>4   </u> cultures developed

    2. some different Indian cultures

      a. Aztecs, Incas, and <u>5   </u>

      b. <u>6   </u> Indians

      c. <u>7   </u> Indians

II. Early Relations with European Settlers

  A. Relations <u>8   </u> at first

    1. Indians helped settlers to adapt

    2. taught settlers to hunt, <u>9   </u>, grow crops

B. Conflicts developed

   1. settlers wanted more <u>10   </u>

   2. settlers thought Indians didn't have <u>11   </u>

      to land

III. Relocation of Indians to <u>12   </u> of the Mississippi River

A. Intended as solution to conflict

B. Problems

   1. money allocated for Indians taken by <u>13   </u> officials

   2. many Indians died on difficult <u>14   </u>

C. Effect of gold rush, increased demand for land

   1. access to gold fields necessary

   2. more land opened for <u>15   </u>

   3. Indians forced onto smaller, less <u>16   </u> pieces of land

Sheep-herding in Monument Valley

IV. Indians' Reputation

   A. Indians thought of as __17_____

   B. __18_____ books often biased

V. Indians' Advantages and Disadvantages in War

   A. Brilliant military leaders

   B. Fought with __19_____ and __20_____

    against guns

   C. Not united

     1. __21_____ into many tribal groups

     2. whites united

VI. Ending of Fighting

   A. Fighting ended by __22_____

   B. Most Indians lived on __23_____

     1. not allowed to leave without __24_____

     2. religious and social __25_____ banned

   C. Government's policy

     1. try to __26_____ Indians into white culture

     2. try to reduce Indian land holdings

     3. changed in __27_____

VII. Indians in Modern America

   A. Mostly live on reservations, though free to __28_____
    anywhere

   B. Have difficulty in larger American culture

     1. not __29_____

     2. not __30_____

   C. Below national average in:

     1. __31_____

2. income

3. 32 _____

D. Indian 33 _____ movement

1. began in 1960's

2. effects

a. government   more 34 _____, less

35 _____

b. Indian leaders more involved in 36 _____

c. Indians have pride in own 37 _____,

history

d. 38 _____ Americans gain appreciation

for Indian culture

Vocabulary Exercise

Find words in the text that have the same word root as the following words.

1. own _____   5. justify _____
2. desire _____   6. tribe _____
3. settle _____   7. compete _____
4. deal _____   8. appreciate _____

Discussion Questions

1. How is the history of the minority or minorities in your country similar to or different from the history of the American Indians?

2. How could the conflicts between white settlers and Indians have been handled differently? How would this have affected the history of the American Indian? How would it have affected the United States in modern times?

3. What, if anything, should be done to improve the situation of American Indians?

12
Potter in the Ancient Way

Maria Martinez had lived all her life in San Ildefonso Pueblo in New Mexico. In modern times, she created the kind of pottery that her ancestors had made hundreds of years before. When she was a child her aunt taught her how to work with clay and shape it into bowls.
5 Although she never used a potter's wheel, her bowls were always completely regular. When Maria was young, the women used to make small bowls to sell to tourists. They worked hard at making the bowls— bowls which were made for use rather than beauty—and then they walked twenty miles to Santa Fe with the bowls. There they lined them
10 up on the sidewalk to sell to people who passed by. However, the women made very little money when the bowls were sold, and gradually they lost interest in pottery making.

The men of the Pueblo did not make pottery at all. The work of the village was divided: the men were farmers and the women did the
15 other work. For example, Maria and her sister had made their house themselves; that was considered women's work. Maria's husband, Julian, was a farmer, but he did not like farming.

When some archeologists from a museum came to San Ildefonso Pueblo to dig in the ruins, there was work there for both Julian and
20 Maria. Julian helped with the digging, and Maria cooked for the workers.

The men dug up a buried village, with many pieces of broken pottery and some wall paintings. When Maria saw the broken pottery, she wondered about the women who had made it. She found small
25 hard pieces of shiny black stones in the ruins and knew that they had been used to polish the pottery, for she used such stones herself. When Julian saw the pottery he noticed the strange patterns drawn on the surface. He began to try to copy them.

The museum director found out that Maria could make beautiful
30 pottery. He wanted to buy her work to sell at the museum. He also asked her if she could mend some of the broken old bowls. When she brought back the first mended bowl, the delighted director gave her many more to do. A new world opened up for Maria and Julian,

a world in which they could really use their creative ideas. While Maria
35 became more and more absorbed with the form and shape of pottery,
Julian thought about pottery decoration.

In that first winter, the couple made and decorated hundreds of
bowls for the museum shop. Then Maria and Julian were offered the
chance to live and work at the museum. They could study the old
40 pottery and make new pottery. For three years they had the time and
opportunity to try to reproduce the ancient art.

Bowl made by Maria Martinez, ca. 1958

Maria began to experiment, to try different clays, to use different
sand. Nothing worked. Then she remembered that once she had
ruined some pottery; it had turned black during the firing. Now she
45 knew the secret of the ancient techniques. When she finally could
reproduce the highly polished black bowls, she had to find out how
to decorate them. To put Julian's delicate drawings on the pottery,
Maria developed a liquid that turned dull black on the shiny black
surface. This black-on-black art became the trademark of Maria Mon-
50 toya Martinez.

The development of this art changed many things in the Pueblo. Farming had been the main source of income. But now both men and women could earn more with their pottery than they had been able to from their farming. Maria taught women how to make the black
55 pottery; she insisted that only the finest work should be done. Julian taught men how to decorate the pottery and how to develop their own ideas of decoration.

Pottery made by Maria and Julian was valued the most by buyers. So that a buyer could be sure who made the pottery, Maria and Julian
60 were asked to sign the pieces they made. Of course these pieces then sold before all the others. Maria and Julian were uncomfortable about this. Competition is considered selfish by Pueblo Indians. They feel that all people should be considered as equal and should help each other rather than try to outdo one another. Maria offered to sign
65 everyone's work, but that just confused buyers even more. Finally, all the work was signed by whoever made it. Many other potters became well-known for their beautiful work. Popovi Da, Maria and Julian's son, and Tony Da, their grandson, also became fine artists; they introduced new ideas such as putting inlays of silver and turquoise on
70 the pottery.

Maria Montoya Martinez

When Maria Montoya Martinez died, she had helped her people recapture the beauty of the Pueblo past. (796 words)

Vocabulary

1. T   **potter:** *a person who shapes dishes, etc., out of clay*
2. 1   **pueblo:** *a type of Indian village in the Southwest, consisting of a group of connected houses built of sun-dried clay*
3. 1   **New Mexico:** *a state in the southwest of the United States*
4. 2   **pottery:** *dishes, etc., made of clay baked in an oven*
5. 5   **potter's wheel:** *round flat rotating disk upon which wet clay is shaped into bowls, etc.*
6. 9   **Santa Fe:** *the capital of New Mexico*
7. 18 **archeologists:** *people who study the life of ancient peoples by studying their buried remains, such as houses, dishes, and tools*
8. 25 **shiny:** *bright; looking polished*
9. 34 **creative:** *new and original*
10. 41 **reproduce:** *make a copy of*
11. 44 **firing:** *baking of clay dishes, etc., in a special oven*
12. 47 **drawings:** *pictures made by drawing lines*
13. 48 **dull:** *not bright or shining*
14. 49 **trademark:** *sign by which a person's work may be recognized*
15. 64 **outdo:** *do better than someone else*
16. 68 **grandson:** *son of a person's son or daughter*
17. 69 **inlays:** *materials which have been set into a surface for decoration*
18. 69 **turquoise:** *a greenish-blue semiprecious stone*
19. 72 **recapture:** *bring back*

Skimming Exercise

1. Where did Maria Martinez live?

2. What work did the men of the Pueblo do?

3. Why did archeologists come to San Ildefonso Pueblo?

4. What did Maria and her husband make for the museum shop?

5. What did Maria Montoya Martinez help her people do?

Comprehension Questions

1. Where was Maria Martinez born?

2. When did she learn how to make pottery?

3. What kinds of work did the Pueblo women do?

4. What did the archeologists and their helpers dig up?

5. What interested Julian about the pottery from the ruins?

6. How long did Maria and Julian live and work at the museum?

7. How did Maria find out the secret of the ancient techniques?

8. What did Maria's pottery become famous for?

9. What became the main source of income for the Pueblo people?

10. Why did Maria and Julian feel uncomfortable when their pieces were valued the most by buyers?

Vocabulary Exercise

Find the adjectives that were used in the text with the following nouns. Some will be in a series.

1. **bowls**
2. **village**
3. **pottery**
4. **patterns**
5. **ideas**
6. **art**
7. **drawings**
8. **surface**
9. **work**
10. **artists**

Organization Exercise

Put the following statements in their correct time sequence.

a. Maria and Julian taught the other Pueblo Indians how to make and decorate the black pottery.
b. Maria's aunt taught her how to make bowls.
c. Maria and Julian made and decorated hundreds of bowls for the museum shop.
d. Maria mended some of the old bowls found in the ruins.
e. Maria was born in San Ildefonso Pueblo, New Mexico.
f. Maria and Julian lived at the museum and studied and copied the old pottery.
g. Maria and Julian's pottery became well-known.
h. Maria made some small bowls and sold them in Santa Fe.
i. Maria and Julian's son and grandson became famous potters.
j. Maria cooked meals for the workers digging in the ruins.

1	2	3	4	5	6	7	8	9	10

Discussion Questions

1. Is pottery made in your culture? If it is, describe it and compare it to the Pueblo pottery in the text.

2. Do you think it is better to have inexpensive things made by machine that everyone can own, or rare and beautiful things made by hand that few people can own?

3. What ancient arts have been lost in your culture? Have any of them been recreated by modern artists?

Writing Exercise

Describe the life of a person in your own culture in the last century. You can contrast that person's life with the present way of living.

IV. Poetry and Song

13
Richard Cory

Edwin Arlington Robinson

Whenever Richard Cory went downtown,
  We people on the pavement looked at him:
He was a gentleman from sole to crown,
5   Clean favored, and imperially slim.

And he was always quietly arrayed,
  And he was always human when he talked;
But still he fluttered pulses when he said,
  "Good morning," and he glittered when he walked.

10 And he was rich—yes, richer than a king,
  And admirably schooled in every grace:
In fine, we thought that he was everything
  To make us wish that we were in his place.

So on we worked, and waited for the light,
15 And went without the meat, and cursed the bread;
And Richard Cory, one calm summer night,
  Went home and put a bullet through his head.
(128 words)

20
25

The poet Edwin Arlington Robinson (1869–1935) grew up in a small town in Maine, perhaps the location for "Richard Cory", and began reading and writing poetry while he was still a child, attending the small local school. Although he decided to be a poet very early in his life, he did not tell his parents, as he thought they would worry about his future. They died before he became famous and never knew their son was one of America's most honored poets. At first Robinson published his poems privately. He moved to New York and supported himself at many odd jobs. In the 1920's he began to become better known and was finally awarded the Pulitzer Prize for poetry three times. (122 words)

Vocabulary

1. <u>12</u> **downtown:** *in the business center of a town or city*
2. <u>14</u> **sole:** *the bottom surface of the foot or a shoe*
3. <u>14</u> **crown:** *the top of the head*
4. <u>15</u> **clean favored:** *good-looking*
5. <u>15</u> **imperially:** *magnificently*
6. <u>15</u> **slim:** *attractively thin*
7. <u>16</u> **arrayed:** *dressed*
8. <u>18</u> **fluttered:** *caused to beat quickly*
9. <u>18</u> **pulses:** *regular movements of the heart*
10. <u>11</u> **admirably:** *excellently*
11. <u>11</u> **schooled:** *trained*
12. <u>12</u> **in fine:** *finally, in short*
13. <u>15</u> **cursed:** *swore at*

Poetry Reading

Read the poem aloud. Pay attention to word stress and sentence stress. Listen to the sounds of the words as you read them. Now read the poem aloud a second time.

Comprehension Questions

1. What did people do when Richard Cory went downtown?

2. What did people think his figure was like?

3. How did they think he was dressed?

4. Did people think he was arrogant?

5. How did people feel when he greeted them?

6. What did the people wish?

7. When and where did Richard Cory kill himself?

8. How did he kill himself?

Poetic Language

A. The words given below are found at the end of lines of the poem.
    Look up the pronunciations in your dictionary. Then find the word
    at the end of another line of the poem that ends with the same
    or similar sound pattern. Write the rhyming word on the line.

    1st stanza   downtown   _____   him   _____

    2nd stanza   arrayed   _____   talked   _____

    3rd stanza   king   _____   grace   _____

    4th stanza   light   _____   bread   _____

B. What kinds of emotions are aroused by these words?

    imperially   richer than a king

    fluttered pulses   cursed the bread

    glittered   calm summer night

C. The poet says that Richard Cory was richer than a king. Make up
    comparisons to complete these phrases in a similar manner.

    poorer than   uglier than

    happier than   sadder than

    sweeter than   lovelier than

Discussion Questions

1. What do you think "he was always human when he talked" (line
    17) means?

2. What do you think "he glittered when he walked" (line 19) means?

3. What does the word "light" (line 14) refer to?

4. What do you think the speaker wants to tell you in this poem?

5. Remember that the speaker is speaking after Richard Cory is dead and for the people on the pavement. Do you believe everything he says?

6. Were you surprised when you read the last line? Why or why not?

7. The last line has a strong impact. Why do you think it does?

8. Why do you think Richard Cory killed himself?

Cloze Exercise

Fill in the blanks with the words given below.

Everyone thought that Richard Cory was the most __1_____
person they knew. He was __2_____ and __3_____.
Although he was very __4_____, he was always
__5_____ to people. They were __6_____ when
he greeted them and said __7_____ __8_____.
Richard Cory had everything possible to make people __9_____
they were in his place. Then one night Richard Cory committed
__10_____ at __11_____ with a __12_____.
People thought that Richard Cory had the __13_____ of
everything, but he really had the __14_____.

**enviable, gun, most, handsome, home, least, slender, good, thrilled, wish,
morning, suicide, nice, rich**

14
Stopping by Woods on a Snowy Evening

Robert Frost

Whose woods these are I think I know.
His house is in the village though;
He will not see me stopping here
To watch his woods fill up with snow.

5 My little horse must think it queer
To stop without a farmhouse near
Between the woods and frozen lake
The darkest evening of the year.

He gives his harness bells a shake
10 To ask if there is some mistake.
The only other sound's the sweep
Of easy wind and downy flake.

The woods are lovely, dark and deep.
But I have promises to keep,
15 And miles to go before I sleep,
And miles to go before I sleep.
(117 words)

20

25

30

Although the poet Robert Frost (1875–1963) was born on the West Coast, in San Francisco, he lived in New England most of his life. Many of his poems are set in New England landscapes, on the kind of small farm surrounded by woods that he himself lived on. Frost tried to use normal sentence sounds in these poems. Until he was middle-aged, Robert Frost was not successful at poetry or anything else. Finally his work was published in England and he became famous. He became the most popular serious poet in America. Other writers also thought he was a fine poet and Robert Frost won many prizes for his work. Americans were very pleased when the much loved poet, then in his 80's, was chosen by President John F. Kennedy to read one of his famous poems, "A Gift Outright", at Kennedy's presidential inauguration. (145 words)

Vocabulary

1. <u>5</u>   **queer:** *strange*
2. <u>9</u>   **harness:** *equipment that attaches a horse to what it is pulling*
3. <u>11</u> **sweep:** *sound of the wind blowing the snow*
4. <u>12</u> **downy:** *light, like duck or goose down (feathers)*
5. <u>18</u> **New England:** *the region made up of the states of Maine, New Hampshire, Vermont, Massachusetts, Connecticut and Rhode Island*
6. <u>29</u> **gift outright:** *gift given with nothing expected in return*
7. <u>30</u> **presidential inauguration:** *ceremony marking the beginning of a president's term of office*

Poetry Reading

Read the poem through twice aloud. Listen for word stresses and word sounds.

Matching Exercise

Match each word in the left column with the word in the right column related to it in the poem.

1. _____ house   a. downy
2. _____ horse   b. harness
3. _____ lake   c. little
4. _____ bells   d. frozen
5. _____ snow   e. village

Comprehension Questions

1. What season of the year is it? How do you know? Pick out the words that give you the clues.

2. Does this poem take place in a city, a desert, or a forest? What is the word that helps you answer this question?

3. What time of day is it? How do you know?

4. What are the different sounds you can hear, mentioned in the poem?

5. How would you describe the way the speaker feels? What words give you clues?

6. Why does the speaker stop in the woods?

7. What causes the speaker to start again?

Cloze Exercise

The editor of a book of poems is discussing the illustration for "Stopping by Woods on a Snowy Evening" with an artist.

"I'd like 1_____ to have an illustration to go with Robert Frost's 2_____ "Stopping by Woods on a Snowy Evening."

"Well, obviously it's evening in the poem. Also, it's 3_____ and there are some 4_____. What else do we need?"

"Let's assume Frost is the narrator, so put a man 5_____ the illustration. And a horse, pulling a wagon with a harness that has 6_____ on it."

"A big horse?"

"No, a little 7_____. And the man, the horse and the 8_____ are next to a 9_____ lake beside the 10_____."

Visualization Exercise

Draw an illustration of the scene in the poem. (You may use information from the Cloze Exercise.)

Rhyme Scheme Exercise

The similar sounds at the end of each line in this poem form a definite pattern. Giving each different sound a different letter, for the first twelve lines the pattern is: aaba, bbcb, ccdc. What is the pattern for the last four lines? Is it the same? If not, what do you think the reason for a changed rhyme pattern may be?

Rhythm Exercise

The poem has a very regular beat, like a chant or a song, with stressed and unstressed syllables. Below are the first four lines with the stressed syllables marked. Look at the pattern and then go through the last twelve lines, marking the stressed syllables. Where are the stressed syllables? How many unstressed syllables are there between the stressed syllables in each line? Now read the poem aloud emphasizing the stressed words. As you read, listen to the rhythm of the poem.

Notice that there is a primary stress (/) and a secondary stress (\ ). The primary stress marks show the normal speaking stress.

Whose woods these are I think I know.

His house is in the village though;

He will not see me stopping here

To watch his woods fill up with snow.

Writing Exercise

Write your own poem in English about a natural scene. Your poem does not have to rhyme, nor is a regular rhythm necessary.

Discussion Questions

1. Sometimes writers use words to mean more than what they actually refer to; that is, the words are used as symbols for other more complicated or abstract ideas. In this poem, the poet may

be using words in just this symbolic way. If "sleep" is used as a symbol for death, see if you can find additional meanings for some of the other words in the poem that would agree with this reading. Does this make the poem more interesting?

2. How do the sounds of the poem change between the first and last parts? How do the sounds make you feel at the end?

3. Do you know any poems in your own language that you can read symbolically? What are they? What symbolism is used?

15 Quince Jam

Edith Shiffert

Amber nuggets packed tightly in their honey
are quince jam from Bulgaria.
Was it made by peasant women in their kitchens
or in commune factories after summer
5 where the hard fruits lay piled
ready to give fragrance to machines?
Did the trees grow in orchards neatly
or twisted and scattered on hills where bees
had to search for the early blossoms,
10 each large, perfect and pink?

My father from Wales required quinces.
His mother had had them prepared for each winter.
Mine, in Octobers, went seeking in markets and found
somewhere each time enough of the rare fruits
15 to please us and her pride.
There were glasses of conserves
and rose color jellies,
and the quarter fruits preserved in their own red syrup
thick with sugar so it barely dripped from the spoon,
20 eaten at special suppers or with preferred guests.
How young was I when I first watched,
peeled a few, stirred a kettle?

Now in Kyoto my breakfast toast this past week
has been spread with thoughts
25 of European hills and homes I never saw,
and of the known disappeared years
coming again with each mouthful,
in the gritty bits of chopped quinces

and the perfumed sweetness melting around them.
30 There was a small tree tended for years
which eventually had a few awesome flowers each spring.
But never fruit. Quinces cannot be forced to come
and we never had them bearing in any of our gardens.

The flavor present has remained familiar
35 to tongue and teeth, and imagination bridges geographies
and affections. The pleasantness
of family Sunday meals eaten
so long ago and unimportant then
is retasted from such a simple thing
40 as a spoonful of preserved fruit on the daily bread,
I realize now an extra reason why my father
an exile in America, wanted this food of his youth.
(308 words)

Filling jam jars

Vocabulary

1. T **quince:** *a hard apple-like fruit used for preserves and jelly*
2. T **jam:** *a preserve made by boiling fruit with sugar*
3. 1 **amber:** *medium to dark orange-yellow*
4. 1 **nuggets:** *small lumps like natural pieces of gold*
5. 3 **peasant:** *one belonging to a low social class, usually farmers, living in the country*
6. 4 **commune:** *a community for group living and working*
7. 16 **conserves:** *jams made with two or more fruits cooked in sugar*
8. 17 **jellies:** *preserves made from fruit juices*
9. 20 **preferred:** *especially liked*
10. 22 **stirred:** *mixed a liquid with a spoon, etc.*
11. 22 **kettle:** *large metal pot for boiling*
12. 23 **Kyoto:** *a large city in Japan, formerly its capital*
13. 28 **gritty:** *containing very small, hard grains*
14. 30 **tended:** *taken care of*
15. 31 **awesome:** *very wonderful*
16. 32 **forced:** *caused to grow by special methods*
17. 33 **bearing:** *producing fruit*
18. 36 **affections:** *tender, kind feelings toward other people*

Poetry Reading

Read the poem through twice aloud. Listen for word stress and sentence stress and the sounds of the words.

Comprehension Questions

1. Where was the writer while writing this poem?
2. What was she eating?
3. What was spread on it?
4. In what country was it made?
5. Where did the author's father spend his youth?

6. Who prepared quinces for him then?

7. Who prepared them for him later?

8. In what ways did she prepare quinces?

9. Were "quarter fruits" eaten every day? When were they eaten?

10. Where did the author grow up?

11. Find three reasons why Edith Shiffert's father wanted to eat quince jam.

Vocabulary Exercise

Fill in the blanks with suitable words from the text.

1. Quince _____ are pink.

2. The _____ of quince jam is red.

3. _____ are the parts of a garden or farm where fruit trees are grown.

4. Quince jellies are _____ colored.

5. " _____ fruits" are fruits cut into four pieces.

6. To _____ is to remove the skin.

7. _____ quinces are quinces cut into small pieces.

8. To _____ is to produce fruit.

Reference Exercise

What do the following words in the poem refer to?

1. <u>3</u>   **it**
2. <u>10</u> **each**
3. <u>12</u> **them**
4. <u>13</u> **mine**
5. <u>15</u> **us**
6. <u>18</u> **their**
7. <u>19</u> **it**
8. <u>22</u> **a few**
9. <u>33</u> **them**

Poetic Language

A. Poetry often changes word order, omits words, and uses unusual words. What is an ordinary coversational way to say: "How young was I when I first watched?" We might say, "I was so young when I first watched." Find the line of the poem which matches each of the following ordinary phrases.

   1. small pieces of fruit in sugar syrup

2. when the quinces were cut up they would smell wonderful
3. my Welsh father wanted quinces
4. when I spread the quince jam on my toast, I think of the hills in Europe where my father grew up

B. In this poem there are several color descriptions: "amber nuggets," "pink early blossoms," "rose colored jellies." Can you use special color words to describe common foods that you eat? What color names do you know in English? Find five new color terms and use them to describe some ordinary objects.

C. Here are some English clichés (phrases which are extremely common, and are always used in the same word order):

1. packed in like sardines
3. scarce as hen's teeth
2. lined up like tin soldiers
4. thick as molasses

Can you find the phrases in the poem which express the same ideas?

1. _____

2. _____

3. _____

4. _____

16

Leaving on a Jet Plane

John Denver

I   All my bags are packed, I'm ready to go,
I'm standing here outside your door,
I hate to wake you up to say good-bye.

But the dawn is breaking, it's early morn,
5   The taxi's waiting, he's blowing his horn,
Already I'm so lonesome I could cry.

CHORUS

So kiss me and smile for me,
Tell me that you'll wait for me,
10   Hold me like you'll never let me go.

I'm leaving on a jet plane,
Don't know when I'll be back again.
Oh babe, I hate to go.

II   There's so many times I've let you down;
15   So many times I've played around,
I tell you now they don't mean a thing.

Every place I go I'll think of you,
Every song I sing I'll sing for you.
When I come back I'll bring your wedding ring.   CHORUS

20 III   Now the time has come to leave you,
One more time let me kiss you,
Then close your eyes, I'll be on my way.

Dream about the days to come,
When I won't have to leave alone,
25   About the times I won't have to say: (193 words)
                                         CHORUS

VERSE

All my   bags   are packed__   I'm   read - y   to   go   I'm
There's so   man - y   times__   I've   let you know   down   so
Now   the   time__   has   come__   to   leave   you

stand - ing   here__   out - side   your door__   I
man - y   times__   I've   played   a - round__   I
one   more time __   let   me   kiss you__   then

hate   to   wake__   you   up   to   say__   good - bye.
tell   you   now__   they   don't mean__   a__   thing.
close   your eyes__   I'll   be on__   my__   way.

But the   dawn   is break -   in'   it's ear -   ly   morn'__   the
Ev - 'ry   place   I   go__   I'll__   think   of you__   ev'ry
Dream   a - bout __   the__   days   to come__   when

tax - i's   wait - in'   he's   blown   his   horn__   al - read - y   I'm   so
song   I   sing__   I'll   sing   for   you__   when I   come   back I'll
I   won't have __   to   leave   you 'lone__   a - bout   the   times__

lone - some   I__   could__   die.__
bring   your   wed - ding__   ring.__
I   won't   have__   to__   say:__

CHORUS

So kiss me and smile for me___

tell me that___ you'll wait for me___

hold me like___ you'll nev - er let me go___

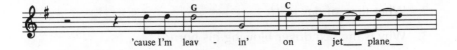

'cause I'm leav - in' on a jet___ plane___

don't know when I'll be back___ a - gain oh

babe I hate___ to___ go___ (There's so)

Vocabulary

1.　T　**John Denver:** *an American singer/songwriter of popular and folk music*
2.　4　**dawn breaking:** *light just beginning in the morning*
3.　4　**morn:** *morning*
4.　5　**blow a horn:** *cause the horn to sound*
5.　10　**hold:** *keep or grasp in the arms*
6.　13　**babe:** *(slang) a girl or young woman*
7.　14　**let you down:** *disappointed you*
8.　15　**played around:** *(slang) dated other people*

Vocalization Exercise

1. CHANTING—The whole class can do this together. Read the song, emphasizing the word stresses. You can clap your hands on these stresses to make them stronger.

2. SINGING—Listen to a record of this song or learn the song from the written music. Many of you may already be familiar with it. Try to memorize the song and sing it to yourself during the day.

Comprehension Questions

1. Where is the singer standing?

2. What time of day is it?

3. Why is the taxi driver blowing his horn?

4. How lonesome is the singer?

5. How is the singer going to travel to the next place?

6. What will he do every place he goes?

7. What will happen when the singer gets back?

8. What does the singer want to do one more time?

9. What does the singer want the listener to dream about?

Grammar Exercise

Make up a three sentence sequence, with one sentence about the past, one about the present, and the last one about the future.

Example: 1) The singer has packed his bags.
              2) He's standing outside his girlfriend's door.
              3) He's going to leave.

1)

2)

3)

Vocabulary Exercise

Write the phrases in the text that have a similar meaning to the following.

1.   <u>1</u>   *I'm ready to go*
2.   <u>4</u>   *the dawn is breaking*
3.   <u>5</u>   *The taxi's waiting*
4.   <u>12</u>   *when I'll be back again*
5.   <u>21</u>   *the time has come to leave you*
6.   <u>24</u>   *the days to come when I won't have to leave alone*

Discussion Questions

1.   Do you know other songs which express similar ideas? What are they?

2.   What feelings does this song express? Are these feelings ones that you have had? Would you express your feelings differently? If so, how?

3.   Do you enjoy listening to American popular songs? If so, what songs do you like?

4.   Compare this song to popular songs of your own culture.

Writing Exercise

What kind of couple do you imagine from this song? Write a short story about how they met.

V. Places to Visit

A Maine harbor

17 Maine Lobstermen

All along the coast of Maine you can see small fishing boats with a single fisherman, or perhaps a fisherman and his family. The boat follows a line of wooden floating markers. These markers are lobster buoys which show the fisherman where he put his traps to catch
5 lobsters. The wooden traps rest on the bottom of the sea until the fisherman pulls them up to see if he has caught any lobsters. Then he takes out the lobsters, puts in fresh chopped fish for bait, and drops the trap and buoy overboard again.

In the summer the fisherman's family will often put up a tent on
10 an island and live there. The fisherman will come back to the island
every night. The family will often have fish for supper; they won't
have lobster as it is worth too much money.

Maine is paradise in the summer. The coastline is beautiful, with
many rocky islands, little harbors, and villages. The islands are covered
15 with delicious berries and the sea is full of wonderful things to eat.
There are dangers for the fisherman, however, as the Maine fogs are
sudden and very thick. Even on a sunny day the fog may come in very
quickly and hide the shore. The fisherman must know where all the
rocks are in the deep water.

20 During the long winter, a lobster fisherman repairs his lobster
traps and his nets, and paints his buoys. Lobstering becomes much
harder and more dangerous in the winter. Ice forms on the ropes and
makes it very difficult to pull up the lobster traps. The ropes may
break and then many of the traps will be lost. Great storms come from
25 the northeast, and many fishermen have lost their lives in the terrible
waves.

Lobstering is a unique American occupation. There are not many
jobs left in which a person can be so independent. The lobsterman
owns his boat; he decides when and how long he will work. Such
30 independence is hard to find in other jobs in America. Many children
want to be lobstermen like their fathers when they grow up. The
children can see that their fathers take pride and pleasure in their
work. The fishermen are proud that Maine lobsters are packed in ice
and flown to all parts of the world. They hope that the small harbors
35 of Maine will be filled with the little lobster boats for many years to
come. (409 words)

Vocabulary

1. <u>T</u> **Maine:** *a coastal state in the northeastern United States*
2. <u>T</u> **lobstermen:** *fishermen who catch lobsters*
3. <u>3</u> **markers:** *objects to indicate a special position*
4. <u>4</u> **buoys:** *floating markers; indicators of objects under the water, or of ship routes*
5. <u>7</u> **bait:** *food put out to catch lobsters*
6. <u>8</u> **overboard:** *over the side of a boat*
7. <u>13</u> **coastline:** *line where the land meets the water*

8. <u>14</u> **rocky:** *made of rocks*
9. <u>27</u> **unique:** *different from other things; special*
10. <u>28</u> **independent:** *able to manage by themselves; not needing help*

Skimming Exercise

1. What kind of fishermen is this article about?

2. Where do they fish?

3. What are two big dangers of the job?

4. What is unique about the job?

5. How do the fishermen feel about their job?

True/False/Not enough information (?)

If a statement is false, rewrite it so that it is true.

T   F   ?   1.   The fishing boats are large.

T   F   ?   2.   Lobstermen live on islands all year long.

T   F   ?   3.   Chopped fish is used for bait.

T   F   ?   4.   Lobsters are caught to earn money.

T   F   ?   5.   Maine has many harbors.

T   F   ?   6.   Summer fogs may hide the shore.

T   F   ?   7.   Traps are lost in the winter because of ice.

T   F   ?   8.   Many fishermen have been killed by icebergs.

T   F   ?   9.   Young people don't want to become lobstermen.

T   F   ?   10.   Maine lobsters are only eaten in Maine.

Comprehension Questions

1. In what part of the ocean are lobsters caught?
2. How are lobsters caught?
3. What are used to show the fisherman where to look?
4. Who often goes lobstering with the lobsterman?
5. What makes the weather dangerous in the summer?
6. What does the lobsterman do with his buoys in the winter?
7. What makes it difficult to pull up lobster traps in the winter?
8. Where do the winter storms come from?
9. Who owns the boat used for lobstering?
10. How are Maine lobsters sent all over the world?

Vocabulary Exercise

Explain the following phrases as they are used in the text.

1. <u>1</u> **boats with a single fisherman**
2. <u>2</u> **The boat follows a line**
3. <u>7</u> **puts in fish for bait**
4. <u>11</u> **they won't have lobster**
5. <u>16</u> **Maine fogs are sudden**
6. <u>18</u> **hide the shore**
7. <u>20</u> **long winter**
8. <u>27</u> **a unique American occupation**

Discussion Questions

1. Compare the lobsterman's life with that of a fisherman in your culture.

2. Is it hard to find independent work in your culture? What kinds of independent jobs are there?

Writing Exercise

Imagine that you have spent the summer with the family of a Maine lobsterman. Write a letter to a friend back home about the life of the family. Describe the family, the place where they live, their daily life, and how their life changes as the seasons change.

18 Hawaii

Hawaii, the youngest state of the United States, is different in many
ways from the mainland states. Its geography and its people are
unique. Hawaii is a chain of volcanic islands, part of a great chain of
islands which stretch across the Pacific. Just who are the Hawaiian
5 people? They are a mixture of the original Hawaiians who probably
came from Samoa long, long ago, and the many immigrants who
arrived later. When the pineapple plantations were being developed
in Hawaii in the 1900's, there were not enough people living on the
islands to do all the work. So immigrants came: the Chinese, Japanese,
10 and the Portuguese formed the largest groups. Some returned home
after working for a few years; many stayed and added to the mixture
of cultures and languages.

*Waikiki Beach, looking toward Diamond
Head*

You can imagine how difficult it was for people to talk to each other. People had to learn little bits of each others' languages. Hawaiian
15 Creole developed from this mixture of languages. Today, many Hawaiian children speak Hawaiian Creole as their first language. However, the Hawaiian language itself is in danger of dying out. There are only several hundred people left who have learned Hawaiian as their first language. They live on the island of Niihau which is isolated from the
20 other islands. English is, of course, the language of instruction in school. Many children learn English for the first time when they enter school.

For many years, Hawaiian customs were looked down on or ignored. Now there is new pride in the old ways. Children are learning
25 the Hawaiian language and the old songs and dances. At the University of Hawaii there is a great deal of interest in the history of the islands and the culture of the past.

Traditional dancer

Visitors to the islands want to see the island paradise as it used
to be. A popular place to visit is the Polynesian Cultural Center. Large
30 numbers of tourists from the Mainland and the Orient arrive in Hawaii
daily. Signs of modern tourism—as on Cape Cod—are everywhere.
Honolulu and its suburbs, a quiet city of about 250,000 about thirty
years ago, is now a crowded area of 800,000 residents and tourists. It
is a favorite honeymoon spot for Japanese couples. Many resorts try
35 to make their Japanese guests feel at home by having signs in Japanese
and employing people who speak Japanese.

As you drive around the main island of Oahu, you can still find
deserted stretches of beach with the famous great waves. Surfers still
ride these waves during the long, beautiful Hawaiian days. But now
40 some of these beaches are closed to the public, and more and more
tourist resorts are being built in areas that were unspoiled. Hawaiians
worry about what will happen to the old way of life. (467 words)

Riding a great wave

Vocabulary

1. <u>1</u> **Hawaii:** *a state of the United States, consisting of a group of islands in the North Pacific*
2. <u>2</u> **mainland:** *principal land mass of the United States on the continent of North America*
3. <u>3</u> **chain:** *number of connected things*
4. <u>3</u> **volcanic:** *of or produced by a volcano, a mountain with a large opening at the top, through which melting rock, steam, gases, etc., escape from time to time*
5. <u>5</u> **Hawaiians:** *native Polynesian people of Hawaii (see #12 Polynesian below)*
6. <u>6</u> **Samoa:** *a group of islands in the South Pacific*
7. <u>7</u> **pineapple:** *type of large dark yellow tropical fruit with thin stiff leaves on top*
8. <u>15</u> **creole:** *a language which is formed by the combination of a European language with one or more others and which has become the native language of its speakers*
9. <u>16</u> **Hawaiian:** *language of the native people of Hawaii; one of the Polynesian languages*
10. <u>17</u> **dying out:** *disappearing completely*
11. <u>23</u> **looked down on:** *despised*
12. <u>29</u> **Polynesian:** *referring to a group of Pacific Islands, east of Micronesia, extending from Hawaii to New Zealand, and to the inhabitants of these islands*
13. <u>31</u> **tourism:** *the business of providing tours, hotels, etc., for people traveling for pleasure*
14. <u>31</u> **Cape Cod:** *a well-known tourist resort on the Atlantic Ocean, located in Massachusetts*
15. <u>32</u> **Honolulu:** *the capital of Hawaii on the island of Oahu*
16. <u>34</u> **honeymoon:** *vacation taken by a newly married couple*
17. <u>38</u> **surfers:** *people who ride on a board over breaking waves near the shore, as a sport*
18. <u>41</u> **unspoiled:** *not yet ruined; in the original state*

Skimming Exercise

Find the underlined words and answer the questions.

1. What kind of islands form the state of <u>Hawaii</u>?

2. What other large immigrant groups came to Hawaii besides the Chinese?

3. When do many children learn English for the first time?

4. How do resorts try to make their Japanese guests feel at home?

5. What can you see as you drive around Oahu?

True/False/Not enough information (?)

If a statement is false, rewrite it so that it is true.

T F ? 1. The geography of Hawaii is different from that of the mainland states.

T F ? 2. The people living in Hawaii are a mixture of many immigrant groups.

T F ? 3. The immigrants originally came to Hawaii as tourists.

T F ? 4. Not all the immigrants stayed in Hawaii.

T F ? 5. Hawaiian Creole developed from a mixture of Polynesian languages.

T F ? 6. Many children in Hawaii speak Hawaiian Creole as their first language.

T F ? 7. The people who speak Hawaiian as their first language live on the island of Niihau.

T F ? 8. There has always been a lot of pride in Hawaiian culture.

T F ? 9. Hawaiian customs and history are being studied at the University of Hawaii.

T F ? 10. All of the beaches in Hawaii are open to the public.

Reference Exercise

I. In the text, "Hawaiian" is used in two ways. Sometimes, it refers to (a) the original Hawaiian people and their language and culture. Sometimes, it refers to (b) the people living in the State of Hawaii. Decide which of the two is being referred to and write (a) or (b).

1. <u>4</u> **Hawaiian**
2. <u>5</u> **Hawaiians**
3. <u>14</u> **Hawaiian Creole**
4. <u>15</u> **Hawaiian children**
5. <u>17</u> **Hawaiian language**
6. <u>18</u> **Hawaiian**
7. <u>23</u> **Hawaiian customs**
8. <u>25</u> **Hawaiian language**
9. <u>41</u> **Hawaiians**

II. Write the nouns or phrases that the following pronouns refer to.

1. <u>2</u> **its**
2. <u>5</u> **They**
3. <u>11</u> **many**
4. <u>16</u> **their**
5. <u>19</u> **They**
6. <u>21</u> **they**
7. <u>28</u> **it**
8. <u>33</u> **it**
9. <u>35</u> **their**
10. <u>39</u> **these**

Summary Exercise

What do you think is the main idea of each paragraph in the text? Write a title expressing the main idea for each paragraph.

Paragraph 1

Paragraph 2

Paragraph 3

Paragraph 4

Paragraph 5

Vocabulary Exercise

Give the verb forms of the words below.

1. <u>5</u> mixture
2. <u>6</u> immigrants
3. <u>20</u> instruction
4. <u>25</u> songs
5. <u>28</u> visitors
6. <u>33</u> residents

Discussion Questions

1. Would you like to go to Hawaii? Why or why not?

2. Do you think it is valuable to keep the old Hawaiian language and customs or is it unnecessary in modern times? What are the values in the old ways of living?

3. Are the people living in your area a mixture of several groups of people? Where did the groups originally come from?

4. Do many tourists come to your area? What effect do they have on the way of life?

Writing Exercise

Imagine yourself in Hawaii as a tourist. Write a letter home describing what you saw and did. Compare Hawaii to your home.

19 Cape Cod

The low land stretches thirty miles out into the Atlantic Ocean, and curls at the tip like a finger. This strange formation was caused by the glacier which covered much of North America thousands of years ago. When it melted, it left behind the long curved stretch of sand.

5   On the outer curve of the Cape are high sand dunes, which are wonderful for children to play on.

The inner curve of the Cape along the bay is very different. When the tide goes out, the water of Massachusetts Bay leaves great stretches of uncovered sand. You can walk far out into the bay, to collect shells 10 or dig for clams. When the tide comes in, the water is very shallow so it is safe for small children to go swimming.

Summer traffic jams are a way of life on the Cape. Route 28, which follows the southern shore, is packed with signs of modern tourism— drive-ins, stores, restaurants, and motels. If you're in a rush, you can 15 take Route 6, a broad, modern highway which bisects the Cape. However, if you are looking for peace and a sense of history, drive along the northern shore on the old Route 6A which goes through unspoiled, quiet villages. (207 words)

Advertisements

The following are advertisements for businesses in the Cape Cod area. When you read an advertisement, you usually do not read every word of it. You look for a specific piece of information—the phone number of a hotel where you want to make a reservation, information about the types of food that a restaurant serves, the hours of a museum, and so on.

Answer the questions that follow the advertisements. You do not need to read every word of the ads; only look for the information that the question asks for. A few words are defined to help you.

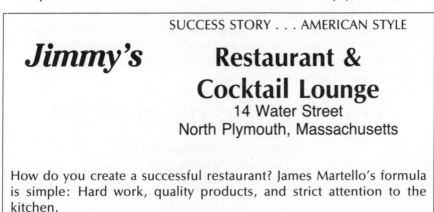

SUCCESS STORY . . . AMERICAN STYLE

Jimmy's **Restaurant & Cocktail Lounge**

14 Water Street
North Plymouth, Massachusetts

How do you create a successful restaurant? James Martello's formula is simple: Hard work, quality products, and strict attention to the kitchen.

Because he has faithfully adhered to this policy, everything at JIMMY'S is delicious—from the appetizer to the dessert. Testimony to this fact is evident when you know that Kiwanians, Lions, and countless other local organizations patronize JIMMY'S.

Other people ride for miles to JIMMY'S for Chicken, Veal, or Steak & Pepper Cacciatore, as well as for Ravioli or Pizzas of all kinds. For me it's JIMMY'S Tortellini in clear Chicken Broth. There's just nothing like it. Or if you prefer, you can have Tortellini with a rich Italian Sauce; and, of course, there's Spaghetti with a variety of Sauces.

In addition to the Italian food for which Jimmy is famous, there is the traditional American variety: steaks, seafood, sandwiches, salads, and special children's plates.

If you fell like relaxing, there's the Lounge, where the drinks are great and the atmosphere restorative.

Luncheon is served daily from 11 AM to 3 PM; dinner, from 3 PM to 11 PM. For delicious food at reasonable prices, choose JIMMY'S.

Vocabulary

1. <u>T</u>   **cod:** *a type of large North Atlantic sea fish*
2. <u>2</u>   **formation:** *something that was formed*
3. <u>3</u>   **glacier:** *huge mass of ice*
4. <u>5</u>   **dunes:** *long hills of sand, piled up by the wind on the seashore or in a desert*
5. <u>10</u>   **clams:** *small, soft-bodied sea animals with double shells that live in sand or mud*
6. <u>12</u>   **traffic jams:** *masses of cars crowded so close together that is is difficult for them to move*
7. <u>13</u>   **tourism:** *the business of providing tours, hotels, etc., for people traveling for pleasure*
8. <u>14</u>   **drive-ins:** *restaurants where customers can order food and eat it without leaving their cars*
9. <u>14</u>   **motels:** *hotels that are convenient for people who are traveling by car*
10. <u>15</u>   **bisects:** *divides into two, usually equal, parts*
11.   **Gov. Bradford:** *Governor Bradford (1590–1657), the second governor of Plymouth Colony, an early settlement near Cape Cod*
12.   **Plymouth Rock:** *the large rock where the Pilgrims, the settlers who founded Plymouth Colony, are said to have landed*
13.   **the American Revolution:** *the war (1775–1783) in which the American colonies won their independence from England*
14.   **cocktail lounge:** *a room with comfortable furniture where alcoholic drinks are sold*
15.   **seafood:** *fish or other living creatures from the ocean used as food*

Comprehension Questions (main text)

1. How is Cape Cod shaped?
2. What is the outer curve of the Cape like?
3. How is the inner curve different?
4. Where is Massachusetts Bay located?
5. What do you find along Route 28?
6. Why would you choose Route 6?

True/False/Not enough information (?) (main text)

If the statement is false, rewrite it so that it is true.

T F ? 1. Cape Cod was formed by a glacier thousands of years ago.

T F ? 2. You'll find sand dunes on the outer curve of the Cape.

T F ? 3. One thing you can do along the inner curve of the Cape is dig for clams.

T F ? 4. Traffic jams are common on the Cape in the summer.

T F ? 5. Taking Route 6 is faster than taking either Route 6A or Route 28.

Skimming Exercise (advertisements)

1. Which town is Jimmy's Restaurant located in?
2. Can you have breakfast at Jimmy's?
3. Does Jimmy's Restaurant serve anything besides Italian food?
4. What is the phone number of the Gov. Bradford Motel?
5. Can you stay at the Gov. Bradford Motel in January?
6. Which period of American history does the Drummer Boy Exhibit deal with?
7. Can you visit the Drummer Boy Exhibit on October 1? In the evening?

Discussion Questions

1. After reading this article, would you like to visit Cape Cod? Why or why not?
2. What is a famous resort area in your country? How is it similar to Cape Cod? How is it different?

20
Adventure in Yellowstone Park

Wilderness! Only three hundred years ago forests and open land stretched from coast to coast across America. Now the National Park System of the United States offers you the chance to experience the wilderness and be awed by the natural wonders of the parks. Yellow-
5 stone Park is one of the best-known parks and is the largest, covering over two million acres. It is larger than Delaware, Rhode Island, and the District of Columbia all put together! The roads wind for hundreds of miles through incredible scenery. A thousand miles of hiking trails invite you into the untouched terrain where you can see bears and
10 many other wild animals.

This excerpt from the *Yellowstone Vacation Adventure Guide* describes the five Yellowstone areas and some of the very special things you can do there.

CANYON VILLAGE. The Grand Canyon
15 of the Yellowstone River is
24 miles of twisting, sheer rock
wall canyon, 1200 feet deep . . .
an awe-inspiring sight. The
Lower Falls of the Yellow-
20 stone, twice as high as
Niagara, cascades down 308
feet, carving an unusual
cleft deeper and deeper into
the colorful red and yellow
25 volcanic rock. Formed in
the ice ages, this spectacular
canyon inspired
the name

Yellowstone. Take the North Rim Drive to the many breathtaking
30 overlooks, follow well-marked trails to scenic vistas. For an insight into the geology and natural history of this magnificent area, be sure to see the visitor center.

HORSEBACK RIDING ADVENTURES. Saddle up! Ride to a Yellowstone adventure few have known—into the depths of the Grand Canyon of
35 the Yellowstone River, on trailwise mounts with an experienced wrangler guide. Take one of several trails

into the hills around Canyon Village. This is great country to
40 explore on horseback. Ask about the many rides available at a Travel and Information Center.
45 Minimum age for horseback riding is 7 years. June 5—September 3.

YELLOWSTONE LAKE. Formed with the violence of earth-shaking volcanic explosions and the force of grinding glacial ice, Yellowstone
50 Lake is today a placid picture of beauty. Its spruce and fir covered shoreline extends more than 100 miles. It reaches to a depth of 320 feet and it is filled with native cutthroat trout. Gulls and pelicans ply its surface and the osprey, Yellowstone's flying fisherman, nests on its picturesque islands. See the lake from the lake—as the captain of
55 your own craft or as a passenger aboard a SceniCruiser. A wide choice of lake activities from remote shore camping to pleasure cruising is available at Yellowstone Lake.

BOAT RENTALS FROM BRIDGE BAY AND GRANT VILLAGE MARINAS. We've got just the craft for you, from rowboats to outboard skiffs to
60 cabin cruisers, where you can enlist your own guide. He'll take you where the big ones are. Depending on the size of the boat, you can take from three to thirteen people in your party. Bridge Bay—June 1— September 15. Grant Village—June 15—September 3.

OLD FAITHFUL. Known throughout the
65 world, Old Faithful Geyser
is truly one of nature's
most magnificent natural
phenomena. It erupts with
predictable regularity,
70 sending about 11,000 gallons
of water into the air and
steam clouds rising hundreds
of feet. It has changed
little in the last 100
75 years. Although Old
Faithful is the most
popular geyser, it is but
one of 10,000 thermal
features in Yellowstone—
80 the largest concentration
on earth. Plan to spend

Old Faithful

some time in this fantastic place. Walk, look and linger along the
boardwalks and paths through the geyser basins. Watch for the
spectacle of an unexpected eruption along the way. Look for wildlife.
85 Explore and enjoy the surroundings.

OLD FAITHFUL INN (Open May 26—September 27). The most famous
of all visitor accommodations within Yellowstone, Old Faithful Inn has
welcomed guests since the turn of the century. It's located in the very
heart of one of the Park's most exciting thermal areas . . . and within
90 two minutes walk from Old Faithful Geyser. The glowing warmth of
the spacious lobby, crackling fire, lovely dining room, Bear Pit Lounge
and snack shop, photo and gift shop, barber shop and beauty salon
have satisfied the needs of guests from around the world.

MAMMOTH HOT SPRINGS. Graceful terraces rise in great stair-like
95 tiers as bubbling hot springs pour out more than 700,000 gallons of
water and two tons of limestone each day. The delicately hued
Mammoth Hot Springs mirror the color of the surrounding area. Yellow
monkey flowers, blue harebell, red fireweed, and the golden tones of
stone-crop add floral color to this exciting thermal area. Explore the
100 neighboring mountains and valleys on horseback. Fish the sparkling
trout-filled streams. And be certain to visit the Mammoth Museum to
view its displays of geology, natural science, and the human history
of Yellowstone.

INDIAN CREEK SCENICOACH TWILIGHT DRIVE. Board a modern
105 SceniCoach for an evening of sightseeing enjoyment. Take your camera
along to capture the wildlife that often feed in the open meadows at
this special quiet time of day. A congenial driver-host will explain the
strange geological features formed by centuries of hot pools bubbling
out dissolved limestone. He will also show you sparkling Glen Creek
110 as it marches past the Golden Gate of Yellowstone. At Indian Creek
you can almost feel the presence of primitive Indians who once lived
here. Leave 7:30 p.m. Return 8:45 p.m. June 7 through September 3.
ROOSEVELT LODGE. The volcanic hills and glacial valleys that embrace
Roosevelt Lodge in carpets of sage, dotted with juniper and aspen,
115 are often missed by the hurried visitor. This serenely beautiful face of
Yellowstone is seen only by those who take the time to discover. And
what treasures there are to find: America's largest petrified forests
standing on Specimen Ridge where they were engulfed by molten lava
some 50 million years ago, Tower Fall with its volcanic pinnacles, the
120 ancient Bannock Indian Trail and rushing rivers and, of course,
Yellowstone's abundant wildlife. Take the time to find this special
place.
STAGECOACH RIDE & STEAK COOKOUT. Climb aboard an authentic
Concord Stagecoach for a ride through rolling sage hills to an open
125 campfire and sizzling steaks. Lofty mountains cast an early evening
shadow as you top off a great meal with home style fruit cobbler.
Delicious! All aboard the stage for a grand ride back. Weath .r willing,
this adventure goes every day from 5:30 p.m. to 7:30 p.m. June 12
through September 2. (1061 words)

Vocabulary

1.	<u>6</u>	**over two million acres:** *about 9,000 km²*
2.	<u>6</u>	**Delaware:** *a state on the eastern coast of the U.S.*
3.	<u>6</u>	**Rhode Island:** *a state on the eastern coast of the U.S.*
4.	<u>7</u>	**the District of Columbia:** *a Federal district located between the states of Virginia and Maryland, wholly occupied by the capital city of Washington*
5.	<u>8</u>	**trails:** *paths through the woods, etc.*
6.	<u>9</u>	**terrain:** *stretch of land*
7.	<u>11</u>	**excerpt:** *section from a book, article, etc.*
8.	<u>14</u>	**canyon:** *long, narrow valley with high cliffs on each side*

9. 16   **sheer:** *straight up and down or almost so*
10. 18   **awe-inspiring:** *causing a feeling of wonder*
11. 21   **Niagara:** *the great waterfall on the border of Canada and the United States between Ontario and New York*
12. 21   **cascades:** *pours (down) in quantity*
13. 23   **cleft:** *space, crack, or opening*
14. 25   **volcanic:** *produced by a volcano*
15. 26   **spectacular:** *attracting excited notice*
16. 29   **breathtaking:** *very exciting*
17. 30   **overlooks:** *places that give views of something down below*
18. 30   **scenic vistas:** *distant views of beautiful natural scenery*
19. 31   **insight into:** *understanding of*
20. 31   **geology:** *study of materials (rocks, soil, etc.) which make up the earth, and their changes in the history of the world*
21. 35   **trailwise:** *familiar with the trails*
22. 35   **mounts:** *horses*
23. 36   **wrangler:** *person who takes care of horses*
24. 49   **explosions:** *violent chemical reactions producing loud noise, heat and expanding gases*
25. 49   **glacial:** *of the huge mass of ice which covered much of North America thousands of years ago*
26. 50   **placid:** *calm; quiet*
27. 50   **spruce:** *a kind of evergreen tree with needles found in the northern part of the world*
28. 51   **shoreline:** *border along the edge of a large stretch of water*
29. 52   **cutthroat trout:** *a type of river fish with spotted, brown skin*
30. 52   **gulls:** *common coastal seabirds*
31. 52   **pelicans:** *large water birds which catch fish for food and store them in long baglike parts under their beaks*
32. 52   **ply:** *travel back and forth*
33. 53   **osprey:** *large, fish-eating bird*
34. 55   **SceniCruiser:** *name of the boat used for sightseeing*
35. 58   **rentals:** *offering boats for rent*
36. 58   **marinas:** *boat docks*
37. 59   **outboard skiffs:** *small open light boats which have motors attached to the back*
38. 60   **cabin cruiser:** *large covered motor boat*

39. 60   **enlist:** *hire*
40. 65   **geyser:** *natural spout of hot water which from time to time rises suddenly into the air from out of the earth*
41. 68   **erupts:** *throws out water, steam, etc.*
42. 78   **thermal:** *naturally warm or hot*
43. 83   **basins:** *hollow places in the ground containing water*
44. 87   **accommodations:** *places to stay overnight*
45. 91   **spacious:** *having a lot of room*
46. 91   **crackling:** *making repeated small, sharp, sudden sounds*
47. 94   **terraces:** *flat level areas cut from a slope, especially one of a number rising one behind and above the other*
48. 95   **tiers:** *numbers of rows, rising one above and behind another*
49. 96   **limestone:** *a type of rock containing material originally from marine bones and shells*
50. 96   **hued:** *colored*
51. 99   **floral:** *of flowers*
52. 104 **creek:** *small, narrow stream*
53. 104 **SceniCoach:** *the name of the sightseeing bus*
54. 107 **congenial:** *pleasant; friendly*
55. 113 **embrace:** *surround*
56. 114 **sage:** *a type of plant with grey-green leaves*
57. 114 **juniper:** *a type of low bush whose leaves remain green all year and whose oil has a pleasant smell*
58. 114 **aspen:** *a type of tall tree whose leaves move in the slightest wind*
59. 117 **petrified:** *turned into stone*
60. 118 **engulfed:** *destroyed by swallowing up*
61. 118 **molten lava:** *hot liquid rock flowing from a volcano*
62. 119 **pinnacles:** *tall, thin, pointed rocks*
63. 123 **stagecoach:** *closed, horse-drawn vehicle*
64. 123 **cookout:** *meal cooked and eaten outdoors*
65. 123 **authentic:** *real; genuine*
66. 125 **sizzling:** *making a hissing sound, as of water falling on hot metal*
67. 126 **top off:** *complete by adding a finishing touch*
68. 126 **cobbler:** *a type of deep-dish fruit pie*

Skimming Exercise

1. What is this an excerpt from?

2. How many areas, facilities, and attractions are described in this reading?

3. In which of the five areas are accommodations described?

True/False/Not enough information (?)

If a statement is false, rewrite it so that it is true.

T F ? 1. There are national parks in the United States larger than Yellowstone.

T F ? 2. One enjoyable thing you can do in Yellowstone is hike.

T F ? 3. The Grand Canyon is a deep canyon with steep rock walls.

T F ? 4. Yellowstone was named for the color of the volcanic rock.

T F ? 5. The horse that you can rent are familiar with Yellowstone's trails.

T F ? 6. Yellowstone Lake was formed as a result of volcanic activity.

T F ? 7. At Yellowstone Lake, you can only rent small row boats.

T F ? 8. Old Faithful is the largest geyser in Yellowstone.

T F ? 9. Old Faithful Inn is one of the best-known accommodations in Yellowstone.

T F ? 10. Mammoth Hot Springs are filled with trout.

T F ? 11. Indians once lived in what is now Yellowstone.

T F ? 12. You can see the forests of 50 millions years ago at Specimen Ridge.

T F ? 13. You can go on the Stagecoach Ride & Steak Cookout every day, regardless of weather.

Comprehension Questions

1. What are the five areas of Yellowstone?
2. Where can you see a waterfall?
3. How was Yellowstone Lake formed?
4. How many people can the rental boats on Yellowstone Lake hold?
5. Which area is famous for geysers?
6. How old is Old Faithful Inn?
7. What does Mammoth Hot Springs look like?
8. About what time do you think it gets dark in Yellowstone during the tourist season?
9. What is Roosevelt Lodge particularly famous for?
10. What do you eat for dessert if you go on the Stagecoach Ride & Steak Cookout?

Cloze Exercise

Two tourists meet at Yellowstone, and one of them starts a conversation.

"Is this your first time at Yellowstone?"

"No, I've been here lots of times. What about you?"

"This is my first time here. I don't really know what to expect. Can you tell me a little about the park and what there is to do here?"

"Well, the park can be divided into   1_____   areas—the Canyon Village, Yellowstone Lake, Old   2_____, Mammoth Hot Springs, and Roosevelt   3_____   areas. Canyon Village, with the   4_____   5_____   of the Yellowstone River and the Lower   6_____   of the Yellowstone, is probably the best known. In fact, the name

"7_____" comes from the yellow volcanic rock there. Yellowstone Lake is also well known. It's a really beautiful area, with many kinds of wild birds."

"What about Old Faithful?"

"Of course, it's known throughout the 8_____ but it's only one of 9_____ thermal features in Yellowstone. That's the largest 10_____ on earth." `

"What did you say the other two areas were?"

"Mammoth Hot Springs and Roosevelt Lodge. The hot springs are on tiered, stair-like 11_____, and 12_____ like monkey flowers, harebell, and fireweed, give the area a lot of color. 13_____ 14_____ is the least known area, but it's my favorite. It includes America's largest petrified 15_____, Tower Fall, an ancient Bannock Indian 16_____, and lots of wildlife. Maybe you should get a *Yellowstone Vacation Adventure Guide.* It tells you about each area, and the activities available there. Here. You can look at mine."

"Hmmm. It says here that you can rent 17_____ and go horseback riding in the Grand Canyon of the Yellowstone, with an experienced 18_____. ... Oh, I see that you can also rent 19_____ at Yellowstone Lake. That sounds like fun, doesn't it?"

"It is—I've done it before."

"I see it tells about Old Faithful 20_____, too. That's very famous. Have you ever 21_____ there?"

"No, I haven't. I usually stay in a cabin."

"This Indian Creek SceniCoach Twilight <u>22   </u>
sounds good, too."

"I've never done that, but you'd probably enjoy it."

"What about the Stagecoach Ride and <u>23   </u>
Cookout?"

"I did that last year. It was a lot of fun. You should try it."

"Well, thanks for all the information. I enjoyed talking with you."

"I enjoyed it, too. Have a good stay at Yellowstone."

Vocabulary Exercise

Match the words on the left with their definitions.

1.	<u>22</u>	_____ carving	a. calmly and peacefully
2.	<u>27</u>	_____ inspired	b. (of a bird) makes a place to lay and hatch its eggs
3.	<u>50</u>	_____ fir	
4.	<u>53</u>	_____ nests	c. very pleasant; delightful
5.	<u>55</u>	_____ craft	d. combined with liquid
6.	<u>80</u>	_____ concentration	e. footpaths made of boards
7.	<u>82</u>	_____ linger	f. shining in small flashes
8.	<u>83</u>	_____ boardwalks	g. a tree of many types that grows especially in cold countries and keeps its thin, sharp needles in winter
9.	<u>84</u>	_____ spectacle	
10.	<u>95</u>	_____ bubbling	
11.	<u>109</u>	_____ dissolved	
12.	<u>109</u>	_____ sparkling	h. shaping by cutting with a knife
13.	<u>115</u>	_____ serenely	i. boat
14.	<u>124</u>	_____ rolling	j. producing hollow liquid balls containing air or gas
15.	<u>127</u>	_____ grand	k. number of items in one place
			l. caused
			m. fantastic public scene
			n. wait for a time, instead of going
			o. rising and falling in long, gentle slopes

Discussion Questions

1. Which of the five areas do you think you would like best, and why?

2. Which of the five areas do you think you would like least and why?

3. Would you like to stay at Old Faithful Inn? Why or why not? If not, what kind of accommodations would you like? Cabins? Camping in a tent? Camping in a trailer?

4. Which activity would you like to do most—horseback riding, boating, going on the twilight drive, or going to the steak cookout? Why?

5. What would be your second choice? Why?

6. Would you like to visit Yellowstone someday? If so, was there something that you read in this excerpt that made you want to go to Yellowstone? What?

Time Record Chart

w/m = words per minute

TITLE	Word Count	1st time		2nd time	
		time	w/m	time	w/m
1 Reading Without a Dictionary	718				
2 Active Reading	641				
3 The American Concept of Time	878				
4 The American Concept of Space	976				
5 The Paper Bag	395				
6 The Man on the Moon	873				
7 Ann Landers	492				
8 The Birdwoman of Falmouth	461				
9 Hopi Indian Doctor	677				
10 Alaskan Arts and Crafts	798				
11 American Indians	862				
12 Potter in the Ancient Way	796				
13 Richard Cory (poem) (poet)	128 122				
14 Stopping By Woods (poem) (poet)	117 145				
15 Quince Jam	308				
16 Leaving on a Jet Plane	193				
17 Maine Lobstermen	409				
18 Hawaii	467				
19 Cape Cod	207				
20 Adventure in Yellowstone Park	1061				

READING SPEED CHART

Number of words:	20	40	60	80	100	120	140	160	180	200	220	240
Time												
1:10	17	34	51	69	86	103	120	137	154	171	189	206
1:20	15	30	45	60	75	90	105	120	135	150	165	180
1:30	13	27	40	53	67	80	93	107	120	133	147	160
1:40	12	24	36	48	60	72	84	96	108	120	132	144
1:50	11	22	33	44	55	65	76	87	98	109	120	131
2:00	10	20	30	40	50	60	70	80	90	100	110	120
2:10	9	18	28	37	46	55	65	74	83	92	102	111
2:20	9	17	26	34	43	51	60	69	77	86	94	103
2:30	8	16	24	32	40	48	56	64	72	80	88	96
2:40	8	15	23	30	38	45	53	60	68	75	83	90
2:50	7	14	21	28	35	42	49	56	64	71	78	85
3:00	7	13	20	27	33	40	47	53	60	67	73	80
3:10	6	13	19	25	32	38	44	51	57	63	69	76
3:20	6	12	18	24	30	36	42	48	54	60	66	72
3:30	6	11	17	23	29	34	40	46	51	57	63	69
3:40	5	11	16	22	27	33	38	44	49	55	60	65
3:50	5	10	16	21	26	31	37	42	47	52	57	63
4:00	5	10	15	20	25	30	35	40	45	50	55	60
4:10	5	10	14	19	24	29	34	38	43	48	53	58
4:20	5	9	14	18	23	28	32	37	42	46	51	55
4:30	4	9	13	18	22	27	31	36	40	44	49	53
4:40	4	9	13	17	21	26	30	34	39	43	47	51
4:50	4	8	12	17	21	25	29	33	37	41	46	50
5:00	4	8	12	16	20	24	28	32	36	40	44	48
5:10	4	8	12	15	19	23	27	31	35	39	43	46
5:20	4	8	11	15	19	23	26	30	34	38	41	45
5:30											40	44
5:40												42
5:50												41
6:00												40
6:10												
6:20												
6:30												
6:40												
6:50												
7:00												
7:10												
7:20												
7:30												
7:40												
7:50												
8:00												

Number of words:	520	540	560	580	600	620	640	660	680	700	720	740
Time												
1:10												
1:20												
1:30												
1:40												
1:50	284	295	305									
2:00	260	270	280	290	300							
2:10	240	249	258	268	277	286	295	305				
2:20	223	231	240	249	257	266	274	283	291	300		
2:30	208	216	224	232	240	248	256	264	272	280	288	296
2:40	195	203	210	218	225	233	240	248	255	263	270	278
2:50	184	191	198	205	212	219	226	233	240	247	254	261
3:00	173	180	187	193	200	207	213	220	227	233	240	247
3:10	164	171	177	183	189	196	202	208	215	221	227	234
3:20	156	162	168	174	180	186	192	198	204	210	216	222
3:30	149	154	160	166	171	177	183	189	194	200	206	211
3:40	142	147	153	158	164	169	175	180	185	191	196	202
3:50	136	141	146	151	157	162	167	172	177	183	188	193
4:00	130	135	140	145	150	155	160	165	170	175	180	185
4:10	125	130	134	139	144	149	154	158	163	168	173	178
4:20	120	125	129	134	138	143	148	152	157	162	166	171
4:30	116	120	124	129	133	138	142	147	151	156	160	164
4:40	111	116	120	124	129	133	137	141	146	150	154	159
4:50	108	112	116	120	124	128	132	137	141	145	149	153
5:00	104	108	112	116	120	124	128	132	136	140	144	148
5:10	101	105	108	112	116	120	124	128	132	135	139	143
5:20	98	101	105	109	113	116	120	124	128	131	135	139
5:30	95	98	102	105	109	113	116	120	124	127	131	135
5:40	92	95	99	102	106	109	113	116	120	124	127	131
5:50	89	93	96	99	103	106	110	113	117	120	123	127
6:00	87	90	93	97	100	103	107	110	113	117	120	123
6:10	84	88	91	94	97	101	104	107	110	114	117	120
6:20	82	85	88	92	95	98	101	104	107	111	114	117
6:30	80	83	86	89	92	95	98	102	105	108	111	114
6:40	78	81	84	87	90	93	96	99	102	105	108	111
6:50	76	79	82	85	88	91	94	97	100	102	105	108
7:00	74	77	80	83	86	89	91	94	97	100	103	106
7:10	73	75	78	81	84	87	89	92	95	98	100	103
7:20	71	74	76	79	82	85	87	90	93	95	98	101
7:30	69	72	75	77	80	83	85	88	91	93	96	99
7:40	68	70	73	76	78	81	83	86	89	91	94	97
7:50	66	69	71	74	77	79	82	84	87	89	92	94
8:00	65	68	70	73	75	78	80	83	85	88	90	93

260	280	300	320	340	360	380	400	420	440	460	480	500
223	240	257	274	291	309							
195	210	255	240	255	270	285	300					
173	187	200	213	227	240	253	267	280	293	307		
156	168	180	192	204	216	228	240	252	264	276	288	300
142	153	164	175	185	196	207	218	229	240	251	262	273
130	140	150	160	170	180	190	200	210	220	230	240	250
120	129	138	148	157	166	175	185	194	203	212	222	231
111	120	129	137	146	154	163	171	180	189	197	206	214
104	112	120	128	136	144	152	160	168	176	184	192	200
98	105	113	120	128	135	143	150	158	165	173	180	188
92	99	106	113	120	127	134	141	148	155	162	169	176
87	93	100	107	113	120	127	133	140	147	153	160	167
82	88	95	101	107	114	120	126	133	139	145	152	158
78	84	90	96	102	108	114	120	126	132	138	144	150
74	80	86	91	97	103	109	114	120	126	131	137	143
71	76	82	87	94	98	104	109	115	120	125	131	136
68	73	78	83	89	93	99	104	110	115	120	125	130
65	70	75	80	85	90	95	100	105	110	115	120	125
62	67	72	77	82	86	91	96	101	106	110	115	120
60	65	69	74	78	83	88	92	97	102	106	111	115
58	62	67	71	76	80	84	89	93	98	102	107	111
56	60	64	69	73	77	81	86	90	94	99	103	107
54	58	62	66	70	74	79	83	87	91	95	99	103
52	56	60	64	68	72	76	80	84	88	92	96	100
50	54	58	62	66	70	74	77	81	85	89	93	97
49	53	56	60	64	68	71	75	79	83	86	90	94
47	51	55	58	62	65	69	73	76	80	84	87	91
46	49	53	56	60	64	67	71	74	78	81	85	88
45	48	51	55	58	62	65	69	72	75	79	82	86
43	47	50	53	57	60	63	67	70	73	77	80	83
42	45	49	52	55	58	62	65	68	71	75	78	81
41	44	47	51	54	57	60	63	66	69	73	76	79
40	43	46	49	52	55	58	62	65	68	71	74	77
	42	45	48	51	54	57	60	63	66	69	72	75
	41	44	47	50	53	56	59	61	64	67	70	73
	40	43	46	49	51	54	57	60	63	66	69	71
		42	45	47	50	53	56	59	61	64	67	70
		41	44	46	49	52	55	57	60	63	65	68
		40	43	45	48	51	53	56	59	61	64	67
			42	44	47	50	52	55	57	60	63	65
			41	43	46	49	51	54	56	59	61	64
			40	43	45	48	50	53	55	58	60	63